Lessons from Turtle Island

Native Curriculum in Early Childhood Classrooms

Guy W. Jones
and Sally Moomaw

Redleaf Press
www.redleafpress.org

Published by Redleaf Press
a division of Resources for Child Caring
10 Yorkton Court
St. Paul, MN 55117
Visit us online at www.redleafpress.org.

© 2002 Guy W. Jones and Sally Moomaw
Chapter opening illustrations by James Oberle
Photographs by David C. Baxter

Redleaf Press books are available at a special discount when purchased in bulk for special premiums and sales promotions. For details, contact the sales manager at 800-423-8309.

Library of Congress Cataloging-in-Publication Data

Jones, Guy W., 1956-
  Lessons from Turtle Island : Native curriculum in early
  childhood classrooms / by Guy W. Jones and Sally Moomaw.
      p. cm.
  Includes bibliographical references.
  ISBN-13: 978-1-929610-25-9 (pbk.)
  ISBN-10: 1-929610-25-4 (pbk.)
  1. Indians of North America—Study and teaching (Early childhood)
2. Early childhood education—North America. I. Moomaw, Sally, 1948-
II. Title.
  E76.6 .J66 2002
  372.19'089'97—dc21

                                                              2002007650

The cover image is an original pastel by James Oberle, who says this about the painting:

> The beat of the Native American drum echoes the heartbeat of Turtle Island, which is also known as North America. Of the seven colors used to create this piece, *red, white, yellow,* and *black* represent the four races of man and the four directions. The seventh color used is *pipestone*.
>
> The turtle represents the living earth. The thirteen circles inside the sacred hoop (the turtle shell) signify the lunar cycles in a year. The thirteenth circle, the drum, is in the center. The sun at the turtle's head and the water, as shown by the thin blue-green line, are essential to all life. The turtle's claws show the connection to all creation.

To my mother and father, Lavorra and Leonard, and to Dakota, without whom I would have never ventured down this road.

Guy W. Jones

To Peter, Jeffrey, and Charlie, the three men in my life.

Sally Moomaw

Contents

Acknowledgments ix

Introduction xi

Chapter 1
Native American Issues in Early Childhood Education 1

Chapter 2
Children—The Most Special Gift 29

Chapter 3
Home Is Where the Heart Is 47

Chapter 4
Families—The Importance of Relatives 65

Chapter 5
Community—We Are All Related 83

Chapter 6
The Environment—Celebrating the Circle of Life 99

Chapter 7
Family Heritage Project 115

Chapter 8
Guidelines for Teachers 133

Index 165

Acknowledgments

We give thanks to the Elders and People of the Standing Rock Lakota Nation for the time from their lives they have given to bring us to this point in our lives.

We are grateful to the children we work with, whose openness shows us the problems of the past and present and points the way for renewed hope for the future. We especially thank the children who donated their work samples to this publication and took the time from their busy days to be photographed: Adrian, Alejandro, Andreana, Bryauna, Bryce, Cammie, Danielle, Elysia, Emmalee, Eoin, Erinn, Hayden, Ian, Inda, Jadarria, Jennifer, Jeremiah, Jordan A., Jordan G., Kellan, Kennedy, Kyle, Madison, Meghan, Monte, Nialani, Samantha, Sydney, Taylor, Yangxing.

We thank James Oberle for allowing us to use his painting, "The Heartbeat of Turtle Island," for the cover of this book, for his moving illustrations, and for sharing a long list of notable Native artists with us. We also thank Dr. Darwin Henderson for sharing his vast knowledge of multicultural children's literature and resources; David C. Baxter for patiently and skillfully photographing the children and helping on yet another book; and Beverly Slapin of Oyate for offering valuable comments on the manuscript and making readily available so many wonderful children's books and other resources for educators.

Special thanks are due to the teachers of the Family Heritage Project, Monica Battle, Lowellette Lauderdale, Amy Mackey, and Melissa Adamson, who incorporated ideas from this book into their classrooms and documented the effects on children and families. We also thank the Arlitt Child and Family Research and Education Center at the University of Cincinnati for its continued support.

We express our heartfelt appreciation to our editor, Beth Wallace, for her insight and guidance, and to the entire staff of Redleaf Press for their unwavering commitment to this project. In addition, we thank Charles Moomaw for his computer and technical support throughout the preparation of this manuscript, as well as for his patience, emotional support, and assistance in obtaining permissions. We also greatly appreciate the efforts of Greg Larson in securing permissions.

Finally, we thank the Miami Valley Council for Native Americans for its ongoing efforts to foster understanding and respect for Native cultures. We greatly appreciate the innumerable American Indian leaders, parents, and educators who have worked tirelessly for generations to secure a future of peace and understanding for all children.

Introduction

This book is a coming together of two authors from very different walks of life to deal with the numerous problems that exist in our educational systems today in the portrayal of American Indian peoples and cultures. Guy Jones, who is Hunkpapa Lakota, is one of the founders and leaders of the Miami Valley Council for Native Americans, an organization whose goal is to foster understanding and respect for Native cultures and to educate the public about Native American issues. Sally Moomaw, who is not Native, is a long-time preschool and kindergarten teacher who also works with future teachers, practicing teachers, and administrators in areas of professional development. Together, the authors examine problems in the coverage of Native American peoples in early childhood and primary programs and suggest appropriate materials and strategies for including Native cultures across the curriculum and throughout the year.

Appropriate terminology is an important issue when discussing groups of people. In the case of people who are indigenous to the Americas, however, there is really no consensus on acceptable group nomenclature. For some time, the term *Native American* replaced *Indian* or *American Indian* in much of the professional literature. Many Native people, though, do not consider *Native American* to be any more acceptable than *American Indian*. In attempting to discuss issues related to various Indian peoples, some authors use the term *Native people,* while others use *Indigenous* or *Aboriginal.* All of these labels, though, face criticism from those who feel they promote an "uncivilized" image. One point of agreement that seems almost universal among people who are native to the Americas is the desire to be referred to by the traditional name of their people. For example, Lakota people would rather be called by that name than *Sioux,* which is not their name for themselves and is actually a French corruption of an Ojibway word implying that they were as lowly as snakes. They also prefer *Lakota* to *Native American,* which groups them with many Nations with different languages and customs. Whenever possible, we have used the traditional tribal names of groups or individuals we are referring to. In some cases, where an author may choose to use the more typical English name for his or her people, we have used both the English name and the traditional name, such as *Navajo* and *Diné.* When it is necessary to refer to groups of people of more than one tribal affiliation, we have used *American Indian, Native American,* and *Native peoples.* We employ the plural *peoples* to remind the reader that the term *Native peoples* refers to many different groups. We are using the term *Native* in the following sense, as taken from *Random House Webster's College Dictionary:* "Belonging to or originating in a certain place; indigenous."

Readers may not realize that American Indian people belong to more than 500 separate Nations. While many Native groups are not recognized by the United States government, many retain a domestic, dependent Nation status as recorded in more than 200 treaties. In recognition of this, in most cases, when referring to specific tribal groups, we have used the preferred term *Nation* rather than the Anglo term *tribe.*

Throughout this book, we have often relied on outstanding children's literature, usually by Native authors, to introduce positive, accurate images of Native peoples to children. (Where appropriate, we indicate the Native background of the author.) It is our view that, with the possible exception of classroom visits by American Indian people, excellent children's literature is the most effective way to counter deeply held stereotypes and help children focus on similarities among peoples as well as cultural differences. The literature serves as a catalyst to extend related activities into other areas of the curriculum.

Unfortunately, children's books periodically go out of print; however, teachers can often find them in libraries or order them from sources that deal with used or out-of-print books, including some of the large Internet booksellers.

Those who work with young children realize that children perceive differences among people much more readily than similarities. For example, a young girl who sees an individual in a wheelchair is much more likely to comment on the wheelchair than the fact that the person is wearing a ball cap similar to the one she may be wearing. Young children also readily notice racial and cultural differences. Skillful parents and teachers help children look beyond differences to the similarities among peoples. The books and materials recommended in this book help non-Native children understand similarities among themselves and Native children while accurately representing Native cultures. Learning about the respectful inclusion of Native American materials in early childhood classrooms helps teachers develop a respect and appreciation for other groups as well. They learn to ask culturally specific questions and not accept curriculum materials blindly. Teachers can apply the recommendations for selecting appropriate Native American books and materials to other cultures and ethnicities as they become sensitized to the issues in diversity education.

Chapter 1 outlines the many problems that currently exist in our schools with regard to Native peoples. Issues involving the omission of Native American materials from the curriculum, inaccurate portrayals or information about Native peoples, stereotyping of American Indian peoples, and cultural insensitivity are discussed at length so that teachers can understand the seriousness and depth of the problems. Chapters 2 through 6 focus on broad topics of similarity among peoples that can serve as unifying themes for curriculum planning: children, homes, family, community, and the environment. Each chapter opens with reflections from both authors on the topic. (Naturally, the names of children involved in school anecdotes have been changed.) Next, issues of cultural similarities and differences are discussed with respect to the chapter topic. Many suggestions of appropriate children's literature and activities follow to help teachers successfully incorporate Native American materials into the overall curriculum. Each literature selection also has recommendations for curriculum extensions.

Each chapter also includes a list of activities or practices that are not recommended, in order to help teachers distinguish between culturally appropriate and inappropriate curriculum ideas. Chapter 7 illustrates the influence of Native American books and artwork on a Family Heritage project undertaken by several preschool and kindergarten classrooms. It shows in action the principles outlined throughout this book and documents their effect on children and families. Chapter 8 is an extensive resource chapter. It includes guidelines for teachers on selecting class guests, children's literature, toys, and materials; an extensive bibliography of recommended children's books; a discussion of problematic children's books; an annotated list of publications to help educators; a discussion of problematic teacher's guides or activity books; a list of recommended recordings by Native musicians; a list of Native American artists whose work is available and affordable to schools or teachers; a selected listing of Native American publications; and a list of Web sites that can provide valuable resources for teachers.

Teachers will note that each literature selection is followed by curriculum extensions, including activities in the areas of literacy, math, science, dramatic play, art, music, social studies, sensory, cooking, and blocks. Many of the activities involve materials teachers can make. For example, in the literacy area, teachers can make charts that relate to the literature selections by carefully printing the words on *sentence strips* (lined paper approximately two feet long and two inches wide) and mounting them on poster board. For writing center activities, they can add *fill-in-the-blank strips,* which are predictable sentences from a book that are preprinted on paper with blank spaces for children to add their own ideas. The fill-in strips can be printed by hand or on a computer. Whatever method is used, the printing should be clear and the letters appropriately formed so that early readers are not confused.

Curriculum extensions in the math area include *grid games* and *path games.* Grid games consist of bingo-type cards used in combination with dice and interesting counters. Path games have movers for each player and dice to roll to determine how many spaces each player may advance. Both are excellent math activities because they focus on quantification and the creation and comparison of sets, using hands-on materials. When assembling materials for these activities, teachers must assess the developmental levels of their students and adapt accordingly. For example, if teachers still have children who put things into their mouths, they should naturally select materials that are large enough not to pose a choking hazard, and so forth.

It is our hope that this book will empower teachers to reevaluate established curriculum; recognize the difference between appropriate and inappropriate materials and practices; and introduce to their children the wonderful books, artwork, and music of Native authors and artists. As Lakota people say, *mitakuye oyasin*—we are all related.

Chapter 1

Native American Issues in Early Childhood Education

Guy's Perspective

For some, knowledge is sorrow. I have a story I'd like to share with the hope that someone can understand the frustration of living in a world not of my own making. As a young boy living on the Standing Rock Reservation, just starting what so many refer to as a formal education, I remember feeling confused from the beginning. Every morning we would start the day with the Pledge of Allegiance and a word of prayer. Following the prayer, we would begin our Bible study. There is one preacher I remember the most, not because of his message or persona, but because of the way he would start his teaching. Every morning he read from the same book and chapter of the Bible to remind us why we were there. I would think to myself, "He really likes this verse."

> For in much wisdom is much grief, and he that increaseth
> knowledge increaseth sorrow.
>
> Ecclesiastes 1:18

We were not to worry, he always told us, because he was there to give us the truth and keep us from grief and sorrow. He would caution us not to seek knowledge, but to let him and the teachers guide us to a better life. Back then, we didn't have the mind to question or even challenge what was being told to us. Still, there are times when I'd like to go back and ask him what happened to those better times we were promised. Indian people on and off the reservation still live in poverty, with despair and suicide rampant among the young.

Today, people say to me, "Don't worry—those days of having another culture's religion imposed in school will never happen again; there are laws now to keep that from happening." As they speak to me, I remember an incident involving my youngest son when he was in kindergarten in a Midwestern, urban school. His teacher held up a sheet of paper and asked him, "What color is this?"

"It's the color of the sky," he answered.

"Wrong," she responded. Holding up another sheet of paper, she asked again, "What color is this?"

"It's the color of the leaves and grass," he answered.

"Wrong," she told him again.

No, she wasn't quoting from scriptures like the teachers I had, but she was still controlling his thinking. He had responded in accord with his Native teachings, to draw relationships to the natural world he was tied to. When he didn't give her the answer she was seeking, she essentially told him that not only was he wrong, but his traditional teachings were also wrong. So I am still concerned about the educational system today.

Sally's Perspective

Steven and Josh were busy working in the art area of the classroom. They had assembled paper, scissors, markers, tape, and glue. As I came over to watch whatever elaborate project they were working on, Josh looked up and informed me that he was making guns. Indeed, he had already assembled two realistic-looking holsters. I decided to probe a bit and asked him why he was making guns.

"I'm a cowboy," he told me. "That's why I'm making guns."

"Why does a cowboy need guns?" I asked him.

Josh thought for a long time. Then he shrugged and said, "I don't know."

His friend Steven, though, seated across the table, knew. Right away he spoke up and said, "A cowboy needs guns so he can kill Indians."

"Why would a cowboy want to do that?" I asked.

"Because Indians are bad," Steven confidently informed me. "Indians kill people. They'll scalp you."

Here I sat with a group of four-year-olds who harbored the same terrible fears and misconceptions as my own generation four decades earlier. What is a teacher to do to counter such blatant racism? Where do children come up with these images and notions? Why aren't we doing more in our classrooms to counter stereotypes and help children understand similarities and differences among peoples? I, too, have concerns about our educational system today.

Why a Book about Native American Issues?

In light of current discussions about embracing diversity in early childhood classrooms, the question could certainly be asked, "Why not a book about diversity in general?" After all, many teachers are trying to move away from isolating groups of people or cultures as topics of study, and most teachers certainly believe that books and curriculum materials about many diverse groups of people should be incorporated into the classroom throughout the year, in all units of study, and across the curriculum. So why isolate Native Americans as a topic for discussion?

There are two critical reasons for focusing on Native American issues in education. The first is the blatant bias with regard to Native peoples that continues to thrive throughout our schools. Long after "Little Black Sambo" images, which are so degrading to African Americans, have been removed from classrooms, we still see blatant stereotyping of American Indian peoples deeply embedded in school culture and curriculum. For example, class dictionaries show degrading images of "Indians" and "Eskimos," and textbooks still contain excerpts from authors such as James Fenimore Cooper, who speaks of "marauding savages." Books and materials for young people mix up and misrepresent Native American Nations, as if they were all one culture, and depict Native peoples as primitive or living only in the past. Meanwhile, our mass media bombards children with cartoons and old westerns, complete with savage images of "wild Indians," while beloved sports teams, many actually representing schools, turn Native peoples into caricatures and mascots. For the sake of all our children, teachers and schools absolutely must acknowledge and begin to rectify these huge problems.

There is a second reason for focusing on the topic of Native American issues in education. By delving more deeply into particular cultures, we can begin to better understand true issues of diversity in general. In looking at the problems so blatantly confronting one group in our educational practices, we can begin to see similar issues among other groups. As teachers, when we learn more about specific cultures, we learn to ask the right questions. For example, if symbols used in American Indian ceremonies are sacred, and Indian people therefore ask us not to incorporate them into art projects with children, are symbols used in some African ceremonies also sacred? Hadn't we better ask? As we learn to ask questions, we also discover where to go for answers. We begin to realize that many of the materials marketed to teachers are not written by individuals from the cultures they attempt to represent. As awareness rises, teachers learn to look more closely at what we teach and what resources we use. Teachers truly need more in-depth information about all cultures. Exploring the issues faced by one group sensitizes us to issues that affect us all.

$ $ $

Guy's Perspective

Recently I ran into a woman I know from the Rosebud Reservation in South Dakota. She's an educated woman, a banker, who has lived in Dayton for some time. She said to me, "I just don't think I can take living here much longer. How do you do it? How do you take the endless stupid comments and questions and never get mad? You must be much more patient than I am. Sometimes I think if one more person asks me if I live in a tipi, I'll just lose it."

My response to her was that I'm not patient, and I do get mad, but you have to think about who it is you're angry with. Otherwise, you're just mad all the time. I told her that you shouldn't get mad at a person who asks you if you live in a tipi because that person is asking you for information. The reason people ask is that they were taught wrong information from teachers. But you can't get mad at their teachers, because they were also taught by teachers, and those teachers were taught misinformation from books. So it goes, on and on.

I told her, "You have to talk to people who ask you if you still live in a tipi. Tell them about your house, because if you change the thinking of just one person, that person will tell another person, and another, and another. You have to do that for the sake of your two boys."

I involve myself with my son's education every step of the way. When he brings his books home each year, I read them. Then I go up to the school and ask the teacher to look at those books. I look at everything. I look at the social studies books. I look at the history books. I look at the health books. I look at all of those things because it is vitally important that the teachers realize that my child is American Indian, and there is a lot of wrong information about Indian people in those books. They need to understand that. For example, the food pyramid in the health books is upside down for Indian people. If we Indian people turn the food pyramid back the other way, more like our traditional diets, we can get rid of much of the diabetes that Indian people now have. When we try to eat like non-Indians, we end up with diabetes.

I believe that as Indian people, we need to involve ourselves with our children's education so that when our children grow up and their children are in school, they don't have to deal with the same issues that we live with. There will be a day when non-Indian children stop asking them if they live in tipis. Reeducating people has to begin today. We need to start telling our story.

$ $ $

Sally's Perspective

I have taught preschool and kindergarten children from diverse cultures for twenty-five years, and for the first fifteen years I had no awareness at all of Native American issues in education. While I have always valued multicultural education, for many years I limited curriculum materials to the cultures represented by the children in my classroom: African American, European American, African, and numerous Asian cultures, including Japanese, Chinese, Korean, Cambodian, Thai, Filipino, Indian, and Indonesian. To me, this approach seemed concrete, real, relevant, and inclusive. Since so much diversity was already present among the children in the program and within the classroom curriculum, I never thought about groups that were not represented, such as Native American or Latino cultures.

I can pinpoint the exact moment when my views about multicultural education changed. I was at a national conference in Denver in 1991 when I happened to wander into a museum where I encountered a time line of the history of the United States that was completely new to me. I read about massacres of Indian people at places like Washita, Sand Creek, and Blue Water. I heard about the destruction of cultures and learned of children taken forever from their families. I was shocked. I consider myself to be a relatively well-educated person, but I had never heard any of this. It was as if every book, teacher, and course I had ever encountered suffered from collective amnesia.

Aghast at my own ignorance, I bought a book about Native American history and read it on the airplane on the way home. Then I bought another book, and another, and another. Eventually, I asked myself what now seems an incredibly ignorant question. Where are Native American people today? Are there any Native American people still in Ohio? After all, I had grown up in northern Ohio looking for arrowheads at state parks and hearing names of towns or schools such as Shawnee, Ottawa, and Miami. Still, I had never met a person who was Shawnee, Ottawa, or Miami, at least as far as I knew. I began to find tidbits in the newspaper about local Native American groups. I visited all of them. Many turned out to be run by European Americans who did not seem to represent authentic Native cultures. Indian people sometimes refer to such folks as "wannabees." Then I attended my first powwow, which was run by a group called the Miami Valley Council for Native Americans, and saw dancers, artists, vendors, and families from many Native nations. I heard music and saw dancing unlike any I had seen before. For me, this was the beginning of listening to Native people talk about their own cultures and learning from them.

In time, I began to explore how to translate this new knowledge into an effective curriculum in the classroom. I found books, recordings, and artwork to share with children, and I began to listen more carefully to the comments they made. Clearly, they had many preconceived ideas of Native American peoples, and their images were not positive ones. I found that in order to help children and be more effective as a teacher, I had to use diversity curriculum more skillfully, not as a didactic tool, but as a means to present positive and accurate images to counter the children's inaccurate ones. Ultimately, I began to collaborate with Native educators to help raise the awareness and understanding of other teachers.

At first, I clearly made some poor choices of materials to use in the classroom. I sometimes selected books written by non-Native authors that did not accurately portray Native cultures. Life is a path of learning for all of us, and in time I found much better resources and learned how to better evaluate curriculum materials. As I watched the responses of the children change as they were exposed to more and more images of Native peoples in the world today, I became convinced that teachers must introduce children to high-quality books and materials from many cultures. This is a critical means to broaden their perspectives and counter the many stereotypes that still exist in society. The children we teach today are growing up in a multicultural world. We must not miss the opportunity we have to help them regard all people positively.

Problems in Today's Classrooms

The educational community has yet to deal with problems related to how Native American cultures and peoples are represented, or omitted, from the curriculum in our schools. While interest in multicultural education continues, issues such as the blatant stereotyping of Native peoples within schools, and their almost total exclusion from curriculum materials, do not even make it to the table to be discussed. Several years ago, when Sally asked her son's literature teacher if her class would be reading any material written by Native American authors, the teacher replied that there were no Native American authors! A social studies teacher volunteered that the students would gain an Indian perspective when they read Chief Seattle's speech (given in 1854). Since the class was currently studying the French and Indian War (1754–63), it would seem that the teacher either was unaware of the involvement of American Indians in that conflict or felt their contribution to history was too insignificant to invite study until the middle part of the nineteenth century. If our teachers remain so ignorant about the role of Native peoples in the entire history of our country, how will non-Native children gain any perspective on the problems that remain to this day?

Problems related to the portrayal of Native American peoples also abound within the early childhood field. While teachers may pay some attention to including African American curriculum materials in their classrooms, little or no thought is given to Native cultures. We have identified four areas of concern with current practices in the early childhood field:

1. Omission of Native American materials from the curriculum
2. Inaccurate portrayals or information in the curriculum
3. Stereotyping of Native American peoples
4. Cultural insensitivity

While the initial reaction of teachers is often that these problems don't exist in their classrooms, as they look closer, teachers typically find that they do. By examining each of these areas of concern, teachers can begin to look more deeply at their own programs and assess aspects that can be changed or improved.

Omission from Curriculum

American Indian peoples are typically ignored in early childhood programs. There are no books, dolls, pictures, puzzles, or other curriculum materials that represent contemporary Native peoples available in most classrooms. When books do find their way into programs, they are often generic, depicting Native American peoples as monocultural rather than as representing hundreds of distinct societies. Such books typically portray Indian people as living only in the past, where children bearing made-up names, such as Little Bear or Indian Two Feet, run around in buckskin vests.

Teachers may not regard omission of Native American images from the curriculum as a problem. After all, the argument sometimes goes, there aren't any Native American children in our school anyway. Teachers out West can worry about including American Indian materials in their classrooms. There are two responses to that argument. The first is that we often don't fully know the backgrounds of the children we teach. While Native peoples live throughout the country, they often don't draw attention to themselves. Sally used to remark that she had never taught any children of Native descent. Then she met a little girl from her class at a powwow. There she was with her fringed shawl, dancing, and she proudly introduced her Cherokee grandfather.

A second point to ponder is that the children we teach today will grow up to live and work in a multiethnic society, one that includes Native American peoples from many diverse cultures. The omission of Native cultures from the curriculum, coupled with generic representations of Native American peoples, leads non-Native children to assume that Indian people don't exist today and had no role in the history of this country. Lack of knowledge leaves children vulnerable to the stereotypical images that they are sure to encounter.

Inaccurate Curriculum

Another problem in the early childhood field is inaccurate curriculum materials related to Native American peoples. Since teachers may lack the background to adequately evaluate materials, they often make inappropriate selections. This leads to misinformation and stereotyping. Later, non-Native children may have difficulties relating to Native American peoples because they lack an accurate historical and cultural perspective. This lack of understanding is clearly evident on some high school and college campuses today, where American Indian students and families protest the misuse of cultural symbols and the stereotyping of Native peoples as mascots, while many non-Native students and alumni claim they are honoring them.

Inaccurate curriculum finds its way into early childhood classrooms via two routes:

1. Curriculum materials written and produced by non-Native people who purport to represent Native cultures, but are not able to do so authentically
2. Societal traditions that perpetuate myths and inaccuracies with regard to Native peoples

Children's literature offers numerous examples of books with Native American characters and story lines written by non-Native authors. Some of these books are written by prominent authors and circulate widely. This is a problem. Non-Native authors frequently misrepresent cultural traditions, and characters may behave in a manner inconsistent with their tribal culture. For example, reviewers Slapin and Seale (Santee/Cree) note the following in *Annie and the Old One* (Miles 1971):

> The traditional dress is not accurate: the hair styles are wrong, the moccasins are wrong. The blanket designs are wrong, the design of the weaving on the loom is not Navajo—or even "Indian." The design on the pot is not authentic. (1998, 42)

Authenticity is important. Europeans and European Americans realize that Europe is composed of many different nationalities and cultures. Therefore, readers would not accept a book about an Italian man described as wearing a Scottish kilt (unless the character was experiencing a huge identity crisis!). Teachers must demand a comparable degree of authenticity in books about Native peoples; otherwise, we perpetuate the myth that all Indians are essentially the same rather than members of more than 500 distinct Nations. Chapter 8 includes a more detailed discussion of problematic children's books.

Curriculum guides with suggestions for "Native American activities" abound. By selecting and isolating a particular art tradition, item of apparel, or celebration, they encourage non-Native children to view Indians as exotic and different, rather than helping children understand similarities among all peoples. Worse yet, they often ask children to reproduce sacred objects, thereby degrading and mocking important cultural and spiritual traditions. Several of these activity books are discussed in more detail in chapter 8.

A further way in which inaccurate information is transmitted in schools, year after year, is through societal traditions, most notably Thanksgiving and Columbus Day celebrations. These two days have become firmly established traditions in classrooms across the country. Not only are children fed untrue or sanitized information, but also they are often encouraged to act out scenarios that probably never happened. A focus on holidays is often referred to in multicultural education as a "tourist curriculum." Classrooms look at an ethnic or cultural group for a brief period each year, usually related to a particular holiday, before returning to a largely European American curriculum. The focus is on exotic differences rather than commonalities among peoples. In a tourist-type approach, Native peoples are highlighted during the Thanksgiving season and are largely forgotten thereafter. Other racial or cultural groups get their turn later, with African Americans "studied" during February, Asian Americans around the time of Chinese New Year, and Latino groups during early May, or on Cinco de Mayo.

There are, of course, numerous problems with this approach to diversity in education, but let's focus on the specifics of Thanksgiving and Columbus Day, since they are the two days that heavily affect Native peoples. Children are taught, year after year, that on Thanksgiving Pilgrims and Indians had a wonderful feast together in peaceful harmony. The truth is, 90 percent of the Native population of Massachusetts died of disease within a few years of encounter with Europeans (Loewen 1996, 80). Pilgrims stole their seed grain, robbed their graves, and exterminated entire villages. In one encounter, 600 Pequots, mostly unarmed women and children, were burned alive when their village was torched (Zinn 1990, 14–15). Thus, for many Native American peoples, Thanksgiving is a day of mourning—for the extermination of peoples, the wholesale theft of lands, the loss of cultures and languages, and the long spiral of grief and despair.

In light of this more complete picture of Thanksgiving, isn't it amazing that we continue to perpetuate the myth of harmony and understanding? In classrooms all around the country, kindergarten teachers dutifully dress children as Pilgrims or Indians, complete with construction paper hats or feathered headbands, for the annual school play. In addition to imbedding inaccuracies firmly in children's minds, this gives them the impression that they can become Indians by dressing up in what is deemed Indian attire. Would teachers dream of dressing up children in blackface for Martin Luther King Day? These annual rites, intended or not, are a mockery of Native peoples and must stop.

While explaining the real history of Thanksgiving might be too graphic and frightening for young children, inaccurate legends can be replaced with new traditions. When Guy asked his Lakota elders for advice to share with teachers, they explained that the idea of giving thanks is part of the traditions of Native peoples. Teachers should focus on the concept of feeling thankful for what we have, they advised, and also emphasize the coming together of families to celebrate unity. It is the view of these elders that the stereotypical trappings of the Thanksgiving holiday, such as the Pilgrims and Indians, should be dropped from the curriculum. Teachers must think about these ideas and decide how they can make meaningful changes in their own classrooms. Some teachers use Thanksgiving as an opportunity to share a class feast. Families contribute favorite foods to share together, and all cultures are celebrated.

Columbus Day is another holiday that grossly distorts history, leaving Christopher Columbus as a mythic hero and ignoring the mass extermination of the Arawak people, their enslavement, the theft of their lands, and the colossal brutality of Columbus and his men. As an example, Arawak people who did not fulfill their quota of gold tribute to the Spaniards had their hands chopped off and many bled to death. In only two years after the arrival of Columbus, half of the Arawak population was dead, and a report from 1650 shows no Arawaks or their descendents left on Haiti (Zinn 1990, 4–5).

Once again we are left with a history that many teachers feel is too gruesome to share with young children. However, this does not mean we need to lie to them. Teachers from middle school through high school and college must begin to present a complete picture of Columbus to their students. Lakota elders emphasize that teachers must be blatantly truthful about Columbus. To do otherwise tells children that it is okay to lie, as long as it is the right lie. Columbus Day is one holiday that these elders would like to see vanish. In the meantime, teachers of younger children can stop reading untruthful stories about Columbus to their classes and instead focus on integrating materials about Native peoples of today into their classrooms. This is better from a developmental standpoint anyway, since young children learn best when material is concrete, real, and relevant (Bredekamp and Copple 1997, 126).

Stereotyping

Many young children already hold stereotypical beliefs about Native American peoples. In a study published by the League of Women Voters in New Brighton, Minnesota, over three-fourths of the kindergarten children gave at least some stereotypical answers to questions regarding Native Americans (Hirschfelder 1999, 3–8). While stereotyping of American Indian peoples is widespread in the media, many materials used in schools also present stereotypical images, and teachers may not have the awareness to adequately screen for these misrepresentations. Such images can creep insidiously into the classroom, perhaps in a class dictionary that depicts a buffoonish "Eskimo" (Eastman 1964, 30) or on a butter container with a picture of an "Indian princess," placed innocuously in the dramatic play area.

The following list describes some of the many stereotypes associated with American Indian peoples. While some of the books listed as examples have been around for decades, they are still widely available in school and public libraries, and many are still sold in bookstores. Some of the examples are very recent publications.

✺ Skin Color and Appearance

Indian peoples are usually referred to as "red," but like all racial groups, their skin colors are varying tones of brown. In addition to being inaccurate, referring to Native peoples as "red" lumps them all together. The skin tone of American Indians varies from Nation to Nation and among individuals, just as with other groups of people. Use of the term "red" when referring to Native peoples feeds into even more derogatory terminology, such as "Redskin." Redskin is an extremely offensive term. It refers to the bounty historically paid by Europeans for the skins of American Indians (Bigelow and Peterson 1998, 58–59).

⚹ Language

Stereotypes of Native American languages involve use of terms such as "how" and "ugh," war whoops, and broken-English language structures. For example, in the well-known *The Indian in the Cupboard* (Banks 1980, 20), the Indian continually speaks in broken English, such as, "I better. You not better. You still big. You stop eat. Get right size." All of these language stereotypes are extremely offensive and perpetuate the idea that Native peoples are uncivilized, all speak the same language, and don't have highly developed languages. Native peoples speak hundreds of different languages.

⚹ Homes

Non-Native children often believe that all American Indian people live in tipis. There is a reason for this erroneous idea. Books, cartoons, and movies typically show all Native peoples living in the past, most often in the tipi, the traditional abode of the plains Nations. For example, *What Can You Do with a Pocket?* (Merriam 1964) shows generic Indians in front of tipis. Some teachers try to counter this by studying the historic abodes of various Native Nations. Few teachers or books, however, show the homes of Native peoples today. Books such as *A House Is a House for Me* (Hoberman 1978), still being sold in bookstores as of this writing, continue to lock Native peoples in houses of the past:

> An igloo's a house for an Eskimo.
> A tepee's a house for a Cree.
> A pueblo's a house for a Hopi.
> And a wigwam may hold a Mohee.

This stanza is clearly an attempt on the author's part to reflect the diversity of Native Nations, and perhaps to counter the prevalent image that all Native peoples traditionally lived in tipis. However, the attempt is flawed because the author portrays Native peoples in the past and not in the present. *A House Is a House for Me* is a clear example of how a well-meant effort to diversify curriculum can go badly astray if all the factors are not considered.

Dress

Once again stereotypes transform all Native American people into members of plains Nations, wearing feathered headdresses as part of their normal attire. Many children's books depict Native peoples in this fashion, while others show children or adults dressing up as generic Indians. Some examples are *Amazing Grace* (Hoffman 1991), in which a young girl dressed up as Hiawatha (Iroquois) sits cross-legged in a stoic pose and wears a full plains headdress; *My First Word Book* (Wilkes 1991), which shows a child dressed as a "chief" in a generic Indian "costume" complete with headdress; *I Like You* (Warburg 1965 and 1993), which shows a child dressed in stereotypic braids, buckskin dress, headband, and feather; the Rugrats book *Be My Valentine* (Wigand 2000), in which an adult dresses in a headband and feather for a Valentine's Day party; *The Golden Picture Dictionary* (Ogle and Thoburn 1976), which includes a white child dressed up as an Indian and Indian characters attacking a fort; *What Do You Do, Dear?* (Joslin 1961), which asks the reader what you should do if you are an Indian smoking a peace pipe with cowboys, and you swallow some smoke; and *If It Weren't for You* (Zolotow 1966), in which the younger child is dressed as an Indian throughout the book. Unfortunately, the list could go on and on.

Warlike

Many young children already view Native Americans as warlike, dangerous, and hostile. The authors of the New Brighton study, which was previously cited, were surprised at the large number of kindergarten children who described American Indians as violent and mean, killing and shooting people (Hirschfelder 1999, 4). Recently, Guy was approached by a young girl who asked, "You're not going to scalp me, are you?" This image of Native American peoples is not surprising given the violent images so often portrayed in movies, in cartoons, and by sports teams who use Indians as mascots, inspiring stadiums full of fans to perform tomahawk chops. Many children's books also depict a warlike image of Native peoples. Sometimes the images are in the background, as is the case in *Will I Have a Friend?* (Cohen 1967), in which a child dressed as an Indian runs around with a tomahawk, hand to mouth in a war whoop, throughout the book. In a book for older children, the "Indian" in *The Indian in the Cupboard* tells Omri, the child character, "Little Bear fight like mountain lion! Take many scalps!" (Banks 1980, 29) While *The Indian in the Cupboard* is a chapter book, some older primary-age children can read it, and it has been made into a movie. Children notice these images, and they leave behind a bias that is hard to erase.

Living in the Past

Another prevalent stereotype of Native peoples is that they lived only in the past. When asked to describe Indian people today, many young children list historical occupations, dwellings, and attire. In other words, they believe that modern-day Indians wear buckskin, shoot bows and arrows, and live in tipis. In the New Brighton study, 69 percent of the kindergartners and 77 percent of the fifth-grade children gave only traditional activities when describing occupations of male Indians (Hirschfelder 1999, 4). Teachers reinforce these misconceptions when they focus their curriculum on Indian dwellings of the past, ask Native guests to come to class dressed in historical attire, or introduce arts and crafts projects that require children to recreate historical Indian dwellings or clothing. Books also reinforce these images. *My First Picture Dictionary* (1990, 179) defines the word *Indian* in past tense and uses a historic picture of Chief Joseph for the illustration: "Indian—a person from any of the groups of people who first lived in America. Indians lived here long before the coming of white people from Europe."

Culture

Non-Native children typically lump all Native peoples together under one culture. This is not surprising since so many books, toys, television shows, and movies do the same thing. This clumping together of cultures in children's minds was evident when a diverse group of American Indians, while on a historic Walk for Justice (1994) across the country, camped in a park in Cincinnati. Several young European American boys approached a Lakota man seated in a lawn chair and asked him to get up and do a rain dance. After politely telling them that he didn't do rain dances, he invited them to show him one of their own dances. In addition to creating generic Indian cultures, non-Native writers often add European elements to them. For example, the back cover description of the beginning reader *The True Story of Pocahontas* (Penner 1994) proclaims, "Pocahontas was a brave, beautiful Indian princess." European cultures had princesses; Native cultures did not.

♪ Music

Hollywood has created stereotypes of American Indian music, along with stereotypes of demeanor, mannerisms, and dress. A typical example of stereotyped music is the fake war chant used by fans of the National League baseball team in Atlanta, students at Florida State University, and others. Rhythmic stereotypes also abound. One often hears a pattern of four beats, with the first heavily accented: "DUM dum dum dum, DUM dum dum dum." None of these stereotypes is heard in the music of any Native cultures; nevertheless, they make their way into "Indian" songs for children. For example, in Silver Burdett's *Making Music Your Own* (1971), a music series that was adopted by many schools and is still available in libraries, a song in the kindergarten volume titled "Playing Indians" (p. 75) contains stereotypes in both the melody and words:

> *Playing Indians is such fun / Let's be Indians now . . .*
> *Did you ever see a Sioux / Ride across the plain . . .*
> *Did you ever see a Crow / Paddling a canoe . . .*
> *Navahos sit in the sun, / Making bowls of clay . . .*
> *Let's pretend we're Iroquois, / Shooting with our bows . . .*
> *Hi-yah! Hi-yah! Hi-yah! Hi-yah! Hi-yah! Hi-yah! Hi!*

One of the problems with school music series is that the editors tend to select one or two allegedly traditional "Native American" songs, often without any apparent consultation from the cultures the songs supposedly represent, and use them as representatives of Native American music. This presents children with an extremely narrow and often inauthentic perspective about Native music. In actuality, American Indian music is extensive, extremely diverse, and continually evolving in the contemporary world, as is the music of most cultures. Some curious anomalies appear in these series. For example, the supposed Hopi "Butterfly Dance" in the kindergarten volume of the Macmillan series *The Spectrum of Music* (1980, 27) has exactly the same melody, with the exception of the last note, as the alleged Hopi "Grinding Corn" song in the first-grade volume of the Silver Burdett and Ginn series *World of Music* (1988, 126), yet the words are completely different. In some music books the only Indian songs that are included are those with vocables (syllables with no apparent meaning)—no words or translations (*The Spectrum of Music*—Level 1 1980, 55 and 59; *Silver Burdett*

Music—Kindergarten 1985, 151). While some Native American music features vocables, when these are the only representations of Native songs included, as is often the case, non-Native children are left with the impression that Indians have no fully developed languages. Perhaps the most blatant and familiar example of stereotyped music is the musical *Peter Pan,* with its "Ugh-A-Wug" song. We cannot excuse blatant stereotypes just because they are considered "art." These images are still damaging to children.

🎵 Depersonalization

One of the most insidious stereotypes of Native American peoples is their dehumanization in books and songs. They are often portrayed as animals in children's books, because authors and illustrators seem to believe that just adding a headdress automatically makes anything into an "Indian." The following are just a few of the numerous books that portray Native American peoples as animals, or vice versa: *The Eleventh Hour* (Base 1993), which shows a tiger in feathered headdress; *Teddy Bears ABC* (Gretz 1975), which includes two teddy bears carrying a headdress; *Richard Scarry's Find Your ABC's* (Scarry 1986), which includes a cat dressed in buckskin shirt and headdress and a raccoon in a headband and feather; *Clifford's Halloween* (Bridwell 1967), in which a dog wears war paint, a blanket, and a headdress and smokes a pipe; *Alligators All Around: An Alphabet* (Sendak 1962), in which one alligator wears a headdress and carries a tomahawk, and another alligator sits stoically, smoking a pipe; and *The Stupids Step Out* (Allard 1974), which shows a dog wearing a headdress. Native peoples are further objectified when they are used as objects for counting in children's songs and counting books. The most widespread example is undoubtedly "Ten Little Indians," which spreads generationally by word of mouth and is perpetuated in music books such as the kindergarten volume of *Silver Burdett Music* (1985, 30). Many adults who grew up singing this song themselves have a hard time understanding why it is objectionable. They must remember that items used for counting are almost always inanimate objects or animals. To group Native Americans with animals or objects is the height of dehumanization. It supports an image of Indian peoples that is undifferentiated by culture and less than human. Just to experience how it feels to be a counting object, try putting your own race or ethnic group into the song. Would any of us sing about ten little white boys, Jews, or African Americans?

Cultural Insensitivity

Omission of Native peoples from the curriculum, inaccurate curriculum, and stereotyping all amount to cultural insensitivity. This is heightened, however, when well-meaning teachers introduce projects that are culturally inappropriate. Teachers may decide to have children "make" an object from a Native culture or ceremony because they equate such activities with hands-on learning. In fact, these activities often demean Native cultures, lead to misunderstanding, and perpetuate stereotypes. It is helpful to analyze various activities in order to understand why they are so problematic. The following are some typical projects often introduced into early childhood programs, along with an explanation of what the objects signify to Native cultures and why including them as projects is inappropriate. Several activity books, all purchased at national early childhood conferences, are discussed; however, teachers will recognize that the types of activities described in these books are typical of those in numerous books sold throughout the country. Teachers should especially note that many of these activities involve sacred objects. When teachers simplify these ceremonial objects, they take away from their sacredness.

🖋 Feathers and Headdresses

This is one of the most common "Indian" activities used by teachers of young children. Some activity books, such as *More Than Moccasins* (Carlson 1994, 51–56), give specific directions for war bonnets or headdresses. They illustrate the somewhat prevalent attitude that children can play Indian, just as they might play cowboy. The important difference is that *cowboy* is an occupation, while *Indian* is a race. Native peoples do not consider making headdresses or using feathers in "Indian" projects to be acceptable. To Native peoples, feathers are sacred. They are often used in ceremonial practice. As a comparison, teachers would not have children make and wear yarmulkes, the traditional rounded caps used by Jewish men to cover their heads in the presence of G-d, as a strategy for understanding Jewish people.

🖋 Peace Pipe

We often hear references to a "peace pipe," and in *More Than Moccasins* children are directed to make peace pipes out of toilet paper tubes (Carlson 1994, 36). The Pipe is so sacred to Native American peoples that it is brought out only for very significant occasions. Although traditional teachings about how the Pipe was given to various Indian Nations differ, all agree on the sacredness of the Pipe. To the Lakota people, the *Chunupa* (Pipe) symbolizes earth, all things that grow on earth, and all things that are on earth. This is represented on the Pipe by leather, feathers, sweet grass, and sage. Indian people consider the term "peace pipe" to be derogatory and feel that class projects that involve the Pipe take away from its sacredness. They therefore regard such activities as highly inappropriate, in the same way that people from other religious traditions would object to children creating representations of their sacred icons.

Sun Dance Skull

To many people, the term "sun dance" evokes images of an exotic Indian dance (or perhaps a particular automobile). Several activity books, including *The Kids' Multicultural Art Book* (Terzian 1993, 22–25) and *Multicultural Festivals* (Weir 1995, 43–45), suggest having children make the buffalo skull from the Sun Dance. The buffalo skull is part of the Wi Wacipi, one of the most sacred ceremonies in the Lakota religion. Needless to say, it is held in deep respect, as are important religious icons in other faiths. Incorporating sacred items such as this into class art projects demeans them. Instead of helping children understand Native cultures, it teaches disrespect for their beliefs and traditions.

Totem Poles

Many teachers introduce totem poles as individual or class sculpture projects. *Global Art* (Kohl 1998, 127) gives directions for making totem poles out of boxes, while *More Than Moccasins* (Carlson 1994, 169–171), *Multicultural Festivals* (Weir 1995, 15–18), and *The Kids' Multicultural Art Book* (Terzian 1993, 30–33) suggest making them out of egg cartons, paper towel tubes, boxes, or paper. Totem poles are still carved by Native Nations in the Pacific Northwest to preserve important teachings, traditions, and historical events and communicate them to future generations. A common phrase in the English language, "low man on the totem pole," conveys a huge misconception. Among Indian people, the bottom of the totem pole is the most sacred place to be since the one at the bottom supports the whole world. While totem poles were never worshiped, a misconception of missionaries that led to the wholesale destruction of totem poles, they are used in important ceremonies. When teachers simplify totem poles by turning them into craft projects, they take away their deep meaning.

Fancy Dance Bustle

Traditional Native American dance regalia should not be equated with a dance costume. The regalia of Native dancers represent a part of their personal identity and also their affiliation with a particular Indian Nation. Dance regalia are considered sacred. Nevertheless, *More Than Moccasins* (Carlson 1994, 48) suggests that children make dance bustles out of pizza boxes and paper plates. Indian children don't play with dance regalia, because they are taught to respect it. Non-Native children also should be taught cultural respect. They should not be encouraged to make or play with Native American dance regalia.

Indian Tom-toms

Teachers err when they assume Native American drums are just musical instruments, as are most drums in European cultures. Thus, they often assemble materials for children to create "Indian" drums. *More Than Moccasins* (Carlson 1994, 83–84) suggests that Indian drums be made from oatmeal boxes. To American Indian people, the Drum is sacred and represents the heartbeat. It is treated with great respect. For example, singers at powwows never leave the Drum unattended. Indian children do not make drums; neither should non-Native children create drums designated as Indian.

Fetish Necklaces

Out of ignorance, teachers may assume that fetish necklaces are just cute pieces of jewelry. *More Than Moccasins* suggests carving the animals out of soap (Carlson 1994, 64–65). The fetishes used in traditional Native necklaces were given to individuals and families and are similar to the historical family and clan crests in European societies. As such, they carry special, spiritual significance. Just as children from one family or clan would not make or wear the crest from another family, teachers should not encourage children to re-create fetishes from Hopi or other Native Nations. To do so contributes to misunderstanding and a lack of respect for cultures not their own.

§ Dream Catchers

Dream catcher kits are commonly sold in craft stores, and *The Kids' Multicultural Art Book* (Terzian 1993, 44–45) suggests making them out of paper plates. It is important for teachers to understand the significance of dream catchers; otherwise, they may introduce activities that mock cultural traditions. Dream catchers are traditionally given to children by their parents, as was the case with Guy, who gave a dream catcher to his young son when he was having bad dreams. The purpose of the dream catcher is to catch the child's dreams in its web so that the bad dreams can melt away in the morning sun. It is sacred to the parent and child relationship and creates special memories. To see the dream catcher reduced to a class craft project takes away from that special significance.

§ Magic Power Shields

A typical stereotype of American Indian peoples is one of mysticism and magic. Some activity books, such as *The Kids' Multicultural Art Book* (Terzian 1993, 18–19), suggest that children create "magic power shields" out of paper plates. Teachers should be aware that many Indian people do not appreciate seeing traditional objects referred to as "magical," with symbols that have special significance to individuals incorporated into class projects. Activities such as this can build barriers between cultures and create animosity. Part of learning to understand and respect various cultures is becoming aware that symbols may mean different things in different traditions. For example, in many Native cultures the clown is considered sacred because he makes you laugh. This is a very different significance than that accorded to the clown in European American society. To refer to "magical power shields" reinforces stereotypes of the superstitious American Indian and suggests that Native Americans are not as advanced spiritually as other peoples.

§ Sand Paintings

Teachers sometimes assume that it is okay to have children create Navajo (Diné) sand paintings because colored sand is used for other art activities. The activity books *Global Art* (Kohl 1998, 125) and *More Than Moccasins* (Carlson 1994, 172) give specific directions for children to make Navajo sand paintings, although the authors acknowledge that they are part of religious or healing ceremonies. Sand paintings are indeed sometimes used as part of Diné healing ceremonies, and Diné elders confirm that they are regarded as sacred in the culture. It may be helpful for teachers to reflect upon how they treat the sacred practices of other religions. For example, while early childhood teachers often incorporate bead stringing into the art curriculum, they do not go a step further and have children make rosaries. Diné sand painting poses the same kind of situation. While working with colored sand may be a fine art activity, teachers should not associate children's art explorations with sacred Navajo sand painting.

$ Pictographs

Another typical preschool art activity, straw blown painting, is transformed into an Indian pictograph project in *More Than Moccasins* (Carlson 1994, 166). Pictographs were a way for Native cultures to pass down their histories to future generations. They were very significant to the culture, as the people would have to determine what events were most worthy of preserving. Thus, while blowing air through straws to move paint is a fine art or science activity for young children, associating a craft project with important Native traditions is not.

$ Face Painting

Face painting is another way in which non-Native children associate Native American peoples with war and violence. *More Than Moccasins* (Carlson 1994, 71) gives directions for war paint and other types of Indian face paint. Recently, Guy was asked to bring Native American dancers, singers, and storytellers into the Dayton schools for a special program. At the first school they visited, the dancers wore regalia but did not have time to paint their faces. The children enjoyed the program and responded positively. After lunch, however, the dancers had enough time to apply paint before the afternoon performances. As the dancers entered the stage, the children became frightened and began to scream hysterically. They screamed so loudly, in fact, that they drowned out the Drum. When the children had finally calmed down, Guy explained the significance of the colors of the paint and described how the manner in which the face is painted tells a story. The dancers then related how each design used in their face paint was given to them in ceremony. When evaluating activities, teachers must recognize that television, movies, and books have all created powerful images for children of war-painted savages. Introducing face painting as an "Indian" activity reinforces these images and detracts from the significance and symbolism of the paint to the individual and the culture.

§ Rattles

As with drums, activity books such as *More Than Moccasins* (Carlson 1994, 78–82) treat Native American rattles as rhythm instruments to be copied as classroom projects. Among Indian people, however, rattles are sacred and are used in ceremony. Thus, while it is fine to use rattles or maracas in the classroom, teachers should not cross the cultural boundary of making specifically "Indian rattles." Rattles have a special significance in Native cultures that should be respected.

§ Kachinas

Kachinas look like exotic dolls to educators who don't appreciate their cultural significance. They appear in the Native American toys section of *More Than Moccasins* (Carlson 1994, 97) and as paper cut-outs in *Multicultural Festivals* (Weir 1995, 11–14). To the Hopi people, Kachinas are sacred and are given for a special purpose. Thus, it is not appropriate to have children make them as an arts and crafts project.

§ Brown Bag Vests

Teachers sometimes have children make "Indian" vests from paper bags. *The Kids' Multicultural Art Book* (Terzian 1993, 16) and *More Than Moccasins* (Carlson 1994, 41) give instructions. Brown bag vests are not sacred, but they do reinforce the "all Indians are the same" stereotype that is common among children and society as a whole. While some Indian peoples wore leather vests, others did not. Another problem with this type of activity is that it conveys the notion that children can become Indian by dressing up. As with other cultures, the apparel of American Indian people is part of their identity, both as individuals and as part of their Native Nation.

When considering activities that involve materials held sacred by particular groups of people, teachers should reflect on the care that other segments of society may use in similar situations. In a recent production of the Verdi opera *Nabucco*, set designers for the Cincinnati Opera Company wanted to include an enlarged text of the Torah, sacred scripture of Judaism, for the backdrop. They realized, however, that this would not be acceptable practice since the Torah is holy text. Rather than pushing ahead anyway, they turned to Hebrew Union College in Cincinnati for assistance. Eventually, a Samaritan text was located and used for the production. Although use of this text was considered acceptable by the Jewish community, it is still considered sacred and therefore must be given to a synagogue at the end of the production rather than discarded (Hutton 2001).

Educators should take note that having children make sacred objects in school, such as many of those cited above, has been ruled by at least one court as transgressing the separation of church and state. In White Plains, New York, a federal judge found a school district in violation of the law for allowing a teacher to have children cut out elephant-head images of the Hindu deity Ganesha, make toothpick "worry dolls," and build an altar for an Earth Day liturgy (Zielbauer 1999; Associated Press 1999).

Goals for Early Childhood Educators

Our goals for educators reflect a deep conviction that learning environments for all children will improve as teachers become more informed about specific issues in diversity. In order to help future generations, we must first inform and guide teachers. Changing the way we teach is never easy. Patterns of teaching and favored curriculum activities and materials can become deeply ingrained. Thoughtful educators, though, never stop learning and improving. Our goals, then, are directed at changing outcomes for children as well as educating and empowering teachers to make appropriate choices of curriculum materials and teaching strategies. The following chapters expand upon these objectives.

Outcomes for Children

§ Understand similarities among all peoples
Children quickly perceive and comment on differences among people. Through appropriate curriculum and sensitive teaching, they can also begin to understand the similarities that link all peoples.

☙ Understand, respect, and embrace differences among peoples

Young children are egocentric. They have a hard time understanding that not everyone views things the same way they do. Adults often seem to have the same problem when dealing with cultural differences. Carefully selected curriculum and teaching strategies can help children feel comfortable with differences among peoples without viewing people from cultures other than their own as exotic or weird.

☙ Develop accurate images of Native peoples

We know that even young children hold inaccurate and stereotypical images of American Indians. Our goal is to counter these images with positive, accurate images that reflect Native peoples today.

Outcomes for Teachers

☙ Learn to accurately evaluate Native American curriculum materials

In most cases, teachers lack the background and education to adequately evaluate Native American content in the literature and materials they use. With increased knowledge and sensitivity to diversity issues, they can make more informed choices.

☙ Develop appropriate strategies for implementing Native curriculum

Teachers often feel that the best way to learn about American Indians is to isolate them as a unit of study. A much more respectful and developmentally appropriate strategy is to integrate Native literature and curricular materials throughout the year, in all units of study.

☙ Develop a resource file of appropriate Native literature and curriculum materials

As teachers begin to discard inappropriate materials, there are many outstanding Native children's books and resources to take their place. Teachers need to be knowledgeable about the materials available and where to find them.

☙ Understand how to recognize and avoid stereotypes of American Indian peoples

Teachers need to become sensitized to the many stereotypes of Native peoples that abound in our society. Only then can they adequately screen materials and terminology that promote inaccurate and negative images.

§ Know where to go to find answers about Native issues in educational environments

Inevitably, there will be some popular book or teaching material that teachers wonder about. Knowing whom to contact to ask respectful questions empowers teachers to continue to improve their teaching materials and practices.

References

Allard, Harry. 1974. *The Stupids step out.* Pictures by James Marshall. Boston: Houghton Mifflin.

Associated Press. 1999. School scolded for Hindu dolls. *The Cincinnati Post,* 22 May, 2A.

Banks, Lynne Reid. 1980. *The Indian in the cupboard.* Illustrated by Brock Cole. Garden City, N.Y.: Doubleday.

Base, Graeme. 1993. *The eleventh hour,* reprint ed. New York: Harry N. Abrams, Inc.

Bigelow, Bill, and Bob Peterson. 1998. *Rethinking Columbus,* 2d ed. Milwaukee: Rethinking Schools.

Bredekamp, Sue, and Carol Copple. 1997. *Developmentally appropriate practice in early childhood programs,* rev. ed. Washington, D.C.: National Association for the Education of Young Children.

Bridwell, Norman. 1967. *Clifford's Halloween.* New York: Scholastic Book Services.

Carlson, Laurie. 1994. *More than moccasins.* Chicago: Chicago Review Press.

Cohen, Miriam. 1967. *Will I have a friend?* Pictures by Lillian Hoban. New York: Macmillan.

Eastman, P. D. 1964. *The Cat in the Hat dictionary.* New York: Beginner Books.

Gretz, Susanna. 1975. *Teddy bears ABC.* Chicago: Follett.

Hirschfelder, Arlene, Paulette Fairbanks Molin, and Yvonne Wakim. 1999. *American Indian stereotypes in the world of children,* 2d ed. Lanham, Md.: Scarecrow Press.

Hoberman, Mary Ann. 1978. *A house is a house for me.* Illustrated by Betty Fraser. New York: Viking.

Hoffman, Mary. 1991. *Amazing Grace.* Pictures by Caroline Binch. New York: Dial Books for Young Readers.

Hutton, Mary Ellyn. 2001. "Nabucco" research pays off. *The Cincinnati Post,* 19 July, 1B.

Joslin, Sesyle. 1961. *What do you do, dear?* Pictures by Maurice Sendak. New York: Young Scott Books.

Kohl, MaryAnn F., and Jean Potter. 1998. *Global art.* Illustrations by Rebecca Van Slyke. Beltsville, Md.: Gryphon House.

Loewen, James W. 1996. *Lies my teacher told me: Everything your American history textbook got wrong*. New York: Touchstone.

Making music your own. 1971. Morristown, N.J.: Silver Burdett.

Merriam, Eve. 1964. *What can you do with a pocket?* Illustrated by Harriet Sherman. New York: Alfred A. Knopf.

Miles, Miska. 1971. *Annie and the Old One*. Illustrated by Peter Parnall. Boston: Little, Brown.

My first picture dictionary. 1990. Glenville, Ill.: Scott Forsman–Addison Wesley.

Ogle, Lucille, and Tina Thoburn. 1976. *The Golden picture dictionary*. Illustrated by Hilary Knight. New York: Golden Press.

Penner, Lucille Recht. 1994. *The true story of Pocahontas*. Illustrated by Pamela Johnson. New York: Random House.

Scarry, Richard. 1986. *Richard Scarry's find your ABC's*. New York: Random House.

Sendak, Maurice. 1962. *Alligators all around: An alphabet*. New York: Harper & Row.

Silver Burdett Music centennial edition. 1985. Morristown, N.J.: Silver Burdett.

Slapin, Beverly, and Doris Seale. 1998. *Through Indian eyes: The Native experience in books for children*, 4th ed. Los Angeles: UCLA American Indian Studies Center.

Spectrum of music, The. 1983. New York: Macmillan.

Terzian, Alexandra M. 1993. *The kids' multicultural art book*. Charlotte, Vt.: Williamson Publishing.

Warburg, Sandol Stoddard. 1965, renewed 1993. *I like you*. Illustrated by Jacqueline Chwast. Boston: Houghton Mifflin.

Weir, Wendy. 1995. *Multicultural festivals*. Illustrated by Kelly McMahon. Santa Ana, Calif.: Wendy's Bookworks.

Wigand, Molly. 2000. *Be my valentine*. Illustrated by Louis del Carmen and James Peters. New York: Simon & Schuster.

Wilkes, Angela. 1991. *My first word book*. New York: DK Publishing.

World of music. 1988. Morristown, N.J.: Silver Burdett & Ginn.

Zielbauer, Paul. 1999. Judge rules school district erred on religion in classrooms. *The New York Times*, 22 May, B1

Zinn, Howard. 1990. *A people's history of the United States*, reprint ed. New York: Harper Perennial.

Zolotow, Charlotte. 1966. *If it weren't for you*. Pictures by Ben Shecter. New York: Harper & Row.

Chapter 2

Children—The Most Special Gift

Guy's Perspective

Growing up on the Standing Rock Reservation, I used to go into the town of Wakpala with my brothers to get bacon and eggs for our grandma. Since she had no electricity or refrigerator, we would stop by her house early every morning, and she would give us the money for the food. I remember the reaction of the clerk when we walked into the store. "Don't you kids touch anything," he would always tell us. "I don't want your dirty paws on my stuff."

As I grew older, I began to wash my hands before I went into the store. "Look," I'd tell the storekeeper. "I washed my hands this morning."

"Let me see," he would reply. Then he would turn my hands over, look at the backs, shake his head as he saw the brown color of my skin, and say, "No. They're still dirty." Hand washing became a compulsion for me, but of course I could never change my skin color.

When my brothers and I would go to the store with my dad, it was different. He worked for the Indian Health Service and was well thought of in the community. The clerk would talk in a friendly way to him, rub our heads, and tell him what fine sons he had. But then, when dad wasn't there, we would go back to being "dirty Indians" and "wild little savages."

Today, Indian children still face discrimination when they go into stores. Clerks watch them closely because they think all Indian children steal. On the reservation, children are referred to in a derogatory manner as "juveniles," as in juvenile delinquent. Nice children, which in general means white, are referred to as "youth." So while the terminology may change, the attitudes do not.

That whole mentality of being called a "dirty Indian" and "wild savage" affected my thinking about myself. I hear people say that children are young and will forget what is said to them. I never forgot. My whole ambition was to be nothing.

$ $ $

Sally's Perspective

During outside time one afternoon, I noticed three boys from my class involved in what I assumed was some sort of superhero play, such as Power Rangers. As I drew closer and began to listen to their conversations, however, I discovered that they were actually pretending to kill Indians. Apparently the cowboy and Indian play so common in previous generations remains with us to this day. Violent play directed toward a particular group of people should always be troubling, but sometimes we become so accustomed to certain play themes that we fail to identify them for what they really are—racism. While I personally know of no teachers who would permit a play theme of Ku Klux Klan members hunting African American or Jewish people, cowboys killing Indians is often accepted as normal, healthy play for children. I recall an administrator once voicing what many may feel, "After all, isn't that all in the past, and isn't that what really happened?"

Fear of an identifiable group of people, in this case American Indians, is not a relic of the past. It is here with us today, and is manifested by children in their expressed fears, which are noted throughout this book, and in their play themes. Of course, our concern as teachers needs to be with the children we are raising and guiding today, and for them hunting down a particular group of people, even in play, is not a historical event. It is real time, because young children live in the present. What I was viewing on the playground was not a Civil War (or Battle of the Little Bighorn) reenactment used to help adults understand a historical period of time. These were children using play to master feelings of fear and lack of empowerment directed toward those viewed as strange and dangerous, in this case American Indians. What tone do we set when we tolerate violent play toward specific peoples? What can a teacher do about play themes deeply imbedded in culture? What should a teacher do?

My concern was to address the feelings that were fueling these boys' play. I toyed briefly with pulling them aside and talking to them about Native American peoples, but I quickly discarded that idea simply because, from my experience, it doesn't work. These boys had formed an image of Indians from somewhere, perhaps television or sports, and my words would not begin to be sufficient to challenge that image. I once had a ten-minute argument with a four-year-old child about whether or not Superman was real. I lost. He had seen Superman flying around on television, and nothing I had to say would alter his schema, or imbedded image, of Superman. I lost the argument but learned from the experience. If you want to change a child's perception, present a counterimage. Create disequilibrium.

In this case, I had a plan. I decided to introduce my children to a book that would show them Native American children today, in a story format that would attract their interest and provide contrasting images to the violent ones that some clearly harbored. I selected "Nanabosho and the Woodpecker," by Joe McClellan. In this trickster story, four young children are playing in the snow, and one decides to climb a tall tree. My three boys were already entranced. "Cool," they said, as Billy, the child in the story, began to climb the tree. Suddenly the branch breaks, and Billy falls to the ground. My three boys gasped, glued to the story line. The children in the book do just what the children in my class would have done. They run for an adult to help, and bring back Nokomis, their grandmother. After she checks Billy to make sure he is all right, Grandma tells a story about how Nanabosho once tried to be a woodpecker and climbed a tree. My class found the story hilarious, and the three boys I had specifically targeted with the book loved it the most. Day after day they asked me to read the book to them. I never mentioned that it was an Indian story; instead, I bided my time and let the images sink in. Then, one day, the time was ripe. I noticed the three boys huddled in a corner pointing at a picture in a book and giggling. The book was called Powwow, and featured a young Native American dancer.

"It looks like you've found something funny in that book," I said as I approached.

"It's this Indian," said the first boy. "He's really stupid."

"Yeah," said the second boy. "Indians are dumb."

"We hate Indians," chimed in the third boy.

This was the moment I had been waiting for, the quintessential teachable moment.

I responded, "I think you might be mistaken about that."

The three boys immediately looked suspicious and guarded. "What do you mean?" asked the first boy.

"Well," I said, "I mean I think you might be mistaken when you say you hate Indians. I was just thinking back to that book about Nanabosho that you liked so much. Remember how many times you made me read it?"

"Oh yeah," replied the first boy, relaxing a bit. "We love Nanabosho."

"Yeah, we love Nanabosho," the other two quickly replied.

"Well," I said, "Nanabosho was an Indian, and so were all the kids you liked so much in the book, like Billy, the one who fell from the tree."

Their mouths literally hung open, and there was a long silence. Then the first boy shook his head and shrugged. "I guess I don't hate Indians," he said.

"Wow," said the other two boys. "I guess we don't hate Indians."

What happened with these three boys? I believe they had an imbedded, fearsome image of Indians that I was able to counter, at least in part, with other powerful images. But it took time. I feel that if I had rushed in with explanations about the races of the characters in the book, the children might have thrown up guards, preventing the new images from seeping in and becoming part of them. The force of powerful literature is in its ability to engage the reader and break through barriers. This is why I believe that a powerful story, dealing with universal human feelings, can go further in reaching children than a more didactic study of groups of people ever can. While I don't believe that these three boys have reached anywhere close to a final resolution of this "Indian" issue, I do believe that they have strong, positive images to recall when they inevitably reencounter negative ones. That is the best I can give them as a teacher.

Building on Similarities

As early childhood teachers, we are already aware of the importance of a child-centered curriculum. We realize that young children understand and know best the things they are familiar with, such as their families, school, neighborhood, and most of all, other children. These things are concrete, real, and relevant for young children, and by and large, we do a good job of organizing curricular materials around these familiar topics. Thus, we share books about children and find that our classes relate to familiar characters, situations, or events and begin to share and write about similar experiences from their own lives. We provide open-ended materials, such as blocks and family figures, and are not surprised when children use these toys to build towns and homes peopled with family units such as their own. We understand the importance of role playing, so dramatic play areas in preschool and kindergarten are stocked with dolls, dress-up clothes, and props that represent home, work, and recreational environments in our communities. Best-practice schools go a step further and incorporate multicultural materials into all of these areas of their classrooms and all of their units of study.

Early childhood teachers do all of these things well and are comfortable with them. Where do we go from here? How do we get even better at what we're doing?

Appreciating Differences

Once we identify topics that are important in all cultures, we have a strong basis for helping children understand similarities. This is certainly the case as we begin to incorporate Native American curricular materials into our classrooms. If we choose well, we find that culturally specific practices, beliefs, symbols, artifacts, and even languages emerge while we are still building on basic similarities. Children learn to understand and appreciate differences while recognizing fundamental similarities among peoples. However, if we choose inappropriate materials, children may instead be taught stereotypes or a dominant-culture interpretation of another culture. Specific ideas for Native American curriculum materials and extensions based on the topic of children follow in this chapter. General guidelines for selecting Native American books and curriculum materials are outlined in chapter 8.

Incorporating Native American Perspectives into Curriculum

Children and Bath Time

Kyle's Bath, by Peter Eyvindson, illustrated by Wendy Wolsak

Wherever they grow up, all children have some exposure to being washed or cleaned. While some children love bath time, others would prefer to avoid it. The child in *Kyle's Bath* is of the latter variety. While Kyle loves to play and get messy, such as by squishing through a muddy garden or making mustaches with his tomato juice, he doesn't like the inevitable bath time that follows, where his mom scrubs him to a shine. When Kyle begins to avoid his favorite messy activities in the hopes that he can also avoid his daily bath, his mother becomes concerned and seeks to remedy the situation.

Kyle is a thoroughly modern child. He watches television, wears jeans and a T-shirt, and bathes in a bathtub. He is also Native American, which is apparent from the illustrations of him and his mother but is secondary to the child-centered story line of the book. Children relate to Kyle because they have had similar experiences with getting messy and bearing the consequences. Because he is first and foremost a child, children accept him, and they identify many similarities between Kyle and themselves. Children also notice differences, however, such as skin tone and physical features. *Kyle's Bath* provides strong and endearing images of a Native American family of today.

Teachers may wish to group *Kyle's Bath* with other books related to bath time, such as *King Bidgood's in the Bathtub,* by Audrey Wood. Grouping books around a similar topic allows children to observe similarities and differences among the characters and situations. For example, King Bidgood loves his bath and refuses to leave the tub, while Kyle tries to avoid taking his bath. This gives children the opportunity to talk about why they like or don't like bath time and what would make bath time more fun.

Writing—Bathtub Stories

After reading *Kyle's Bath* and other books about bath time, children often relate their own favorite experiences about bathing. They may also identify with Kyle and talk about things they don't like. This activity directs those conversations into the writing venue. Children can write about their bath time experiences in small books shaped like bathtubs. Several blank pages inside provide space for printing or for an adult to write what the child dictates. The bathtub story writing can be introduced as a special activity or placed in the writing center of the classroom.

Lucy's Bathtub Book

Child	Like ☺	Don't Like ☹
Kayla	goldfish	dogs
Jonathan	writing	bath
Amber	Barbies	guns
Sarah	chicken pie	spaghetti
Antonio	Pokemon	real guns
Aaron	dinosaurs	showers
Maria	dinosaurs	
Jianfei	crocodiles	bugs
Steve	Pokemon	milk
Audrey	pizza	
Carina	dogs	monsters
Mark	bath	hair wash
Sasha	spaghetti	
Tiffany	bunnies	bugs

Reading and Writing— Likes and Don't Likes

While Kyle is not fond of his bath, there are many things he does like. The author and illustrator create long lists of his favorite things. All children have many things in their lives that they especially like, as well as some things they don't like. For this activity, each child's name is listed along the side of a large piece of chart paper (lined) or easel paper (unlined). Two columns are labeled "Like" and "Don't Like" at the top of the paper. After discussing some of the things Kyle likes and doesn't like, children can dictate or write one thing they like and one thing they don't like for inclusion on the chart. Children enjoy returning to the chart to compare notes on their likes and dislikes. Some children may wish to compose lists of likes and dislikes on paper in the writing center or in their journals.

Sensory Table—Bathing Multicultural Baby Dolls

Bathing babies is a common activity in preschool. By using multicultural dolls and coordinating this sensory table activity with *Kyle's Bath*, teachers help children draw relationships about the similarities among peoples. Perhaps a parent with a baby would be willing to come to class and demonstrate how he or she bathes the baby.

Math—Bathtub Game

The bathtub is a prominent feature in *Kyle's Bath*. This math game builds on that association with the book. Each player has an inexpensive plastic bathtub, sold as soap holders in discount department stores and pharmacies, to fill with multicultural toy figures, such as Duplo World People. Players take turns rolling a 1–3 or 1–6 die and placing a corresponding number of toy people in their bathtubs. When all of the people have been used, children can compare how many each has in his or her bathtub. This is an excellent math activity for young children because it focuses on quantification and the creation and comparison of sets, using hands-on materials. For older children who are working on addition, tiny multicultural babies or

laminated baby stickers can be substituted for the people figures. Children can roll two dice and add them together before placing the babies in the bathtub. While this game focuses on math concepts, the use of multicultural figures, as well as the close association with *Kyle's Bath*, helps reinforce the concept of similarities among peoples.

Note that some brands of people figurines contain stereotypical images, such as American Indians with tomahawks or headdresses, which should, of course, be avoided. Select carefully when purchasing multicultural toys for your school or classroom.

Children and Shoes

Where Did You Get Your Moccasins?
by Bernelda Wheeler, illustrated by Herman Bekkering

Early childhood teachers, parents, and administrators are
keenly aware of how interested children are in their shoes.
These two excellent children's books build on that interest,
but in this case, the main characters are Native children. In
Where Did You Get Your Moccasins, by Cree/Saulteaux author
Bernelda Wheeler, a child brings a pair of moccasins to
school to share during "Show and Tell." He explains how
his Kookum, or grandma, made the moccasins. The "add-
on" style of the text helps beginning readers predict what
will come next. While the illustrations show a modern
Native child in a multicultural classroom, they also show his grandmother tanning deer hide and making the moccasins in a traditional way.
The ending is delightful. When the teacher asks where his Kookum got the
beads, we expect to hear of some traditional source. Instead, the child replies
with a big smile, "From the store." This is a modern child whose family maintains important cultural traditions.

Two Pairs of Shoes, by Esther Sanderson,
illustrated by David Beyer

Two Pairs of Shoes, by Esther Sanderson from
the Pas Reserve in Manitoba, introduces us to
a Native American girl who receives two special pairs of shoes for her birthday: black
patent-leather shoes from her mother and
beautifully beaded moccasins from her
grandmother. Again we see a Native family
of today maintaining cultural traditions.
Children readily identify with Maggie, the
main character in the book, because of her birthday
excitement and her special shoes. They quickly begin to talk about their own

birthdays and their own favorite shoes. Both books are successful in helping children understand similarities but also provide a window into cultural differences. Teachers might couple these two books with other books about shoes, such as *Red Dancing Shoes,* by Denise Lewis Patrick, which features African American characters, and *Shoes, Shoes, Shoes,* by Ann Morris, which shows shoes from around the world.

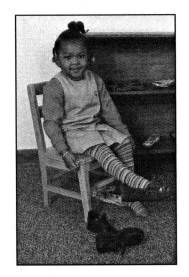

Dramatic Play—Shoe Store

A multicultural shoe store, incorporated into the dramatic play area, gives children the opportunity to compare various types of shoes and notice both similarities and differences. Children quickly discover that people from many different cultures all have some way of covering and protecting their feet. This is a pronounced similarity. On the other hand, shoes from various cultures also have interesting differences, including the materials they are made from and the decorations. Parents may be able to help in assembling a variety of types of shoes. Moccasins are still popular footwear, so parents may have "hand-me-downs" from older children. They may have friends or acquaintances from other countries who will donate shoes to the school. Some early childhood catalogues are now beginning to feature shoes from other cultures. International festivals are also a good place to look for inexpensive shoes or slippers, as are stores in ethnic neighborhoods.

Math—Shoe Collection

Several excellent math activities capitalize on the similarities and differences among shoes. The shoe collection is an assortment of small novelty shoes that children can group and classify by a variety of attributes, such as color,

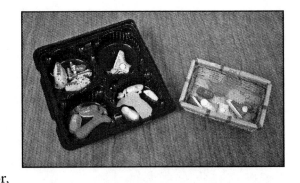

type of shoe, material, or size. The shoes can be found in party supply stores, craft stores, or novelty stores and catalogues. Look for tiny moccasins to include in your collection. This helps children reinforce similarities among peoples.

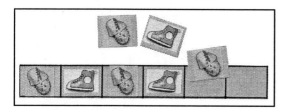

Math—Shoe Patterns

Children can use the novelty shoes, pictures of shoes, or real shoes to create patterns. The teacher might start by creating a pattern with the shoes, such as moccasin, sneaker, moccasin, sneaker. Children can help extend the pattern and then begin to create their own patterns.

Math—Shoe Graph

A shoe graph provides children with the opportunity to group their shoes by a particular attribute, organize the data, and quantify and compare the results. For example, the class might graph their shoes by color, type of fastener, or type of shoe. Teachers can divide poster board into columns with a label and illustration for the sorting attribute at the bottom of each column. Tags with each child's name can then be placed in the appropriate column. Graphing shoes helps point out similarities and differences. For example, if a class is graphing shoes by color, a white moccasin might end up in the same column as a white sandal. Although the shoes are different, they share a common attribute.

What color are our shoes?

	Karen				
	Michael				Kim
	Nancy		Isabelle		David
Jared	Sanjay	Charlie	Crystal	Andre	Sheldon
Hayley	Iris	Wendy	Ping	Joseph	Greg
red	brown	white	pink	blue	black

Art—Sewing with Beads

Since both *Where Did You Get Your Moccasins* and *Two Pairs of Shoes* feature moccasins with elaborate beadwork, children may also be interested in sewing with beads. While tiny seed beads and leather are too difficult for young children to work with, they can sew larger pony beads onto burlap using large plastic safety needles and yarn. For ease of use, cut the burlap into 7-inch squares and mount the pieces on embroidery hoops. This keeps the fabric taut while children sew.

Teachers should not encourage children to re-create so-called Indian patterns with the beads. Let them sew in their own way. If older children wish to create patterns or forms, encourage them to think about designs or symbols that are meaningful to them.

Science—Shoe Prints

This activity allows children to construct the relationship

between the soles of different types of shoes and the impression they create in moist sand. Place a variety of types of shoes, such as sneakers, sandals, high heels, boots, and moccasins, next to a tub of moist sand. Children can press the shoes into the sand and observe the shape of the indentation created by each type of shoe.

Teachers should be careful not to give children the misconception that moccasins are the only shoes worn by Native peoples today. Most of us wear many different types of shoes, and this is certainly the case for American Indians as well. While moccasins originated with Native peoples, the moccasin-style shoe is now worn by people in many parts of the world.

Children and Pets

The Good Luck Cat, by Joy Harjo, illustrated by Paul Lee

Many books about Native American peoples written for primary-age children are set in the past, as though Indian people do not exist today. They frequently feature characters with fake Indian names, such as Bright Stars, and attempt to represent a globalized image of Native culture that never existed. *The Good Luck Cat* is a welcome departure from such books. Written by Muskogee (Creek) author Joy Harjo, it features a Native child of today who has lost her cat. Specific aspects of her culture are clearly apparent in both the text and illustrations, such as an incident where she locks the cat in the trunk of her family's car so she can sneak it into a powwow. Children readily identify with the main character because many of them also have pets that they love. Children also notice that the child in the story lives in a modern home complete with washer and dryer. She has a loving family and goes to school, just like they do. Thus, the book successfully counters Indian stereotypes while providing a window through which the reader can see a Native family in an urban environment.

Writing—Pet Stories

Most children have had some experience with pets. They may have pets of their own, see pets at their friends' homes, or notice pets in their neighborhood. For this activity, children can write their own pet stories. They may choose to write about a real experience with a pet or create a fictional story. Children can illustrate their stories and share them with the class.

Math—Lost Cat Game

This path game can be used for addition or subtraction. The game board, which is made of colored poster board, 22 by 22 inches, features a path made of 1-inch round stickers and trap spaces that coordinate with the story line of *The Good Luck Cat:*

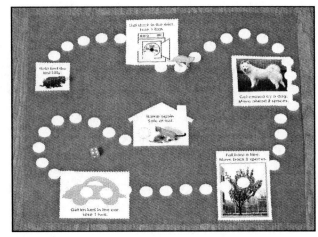

> Get stuck in the dryer. Lose 1 turn.
> Get chased by a dog. Move ahead 2 spaces.
> Fall from a tree. Move back 1 space.
> Get scared. Run ahead 3 spaces.
> Get locked in the car. Lose 1 turn.

Stickers are used to illustrate the trap spaces. The beginning of the game features a sticker of a cat, and the final space says, "Home again. Safe at last." The movers are small toy cats (see left).

To play the game, children roll two dice. They can add the dice together to determine how many spaces to move their cat or subtract the smaller number on the dice from the larger number before moving.

Children and Toys

Baseball Bats for Christmas by Michael Arvaarluk Kusugak, with art by Vladyana Krykorka

Baseball Bats for Christmas is a charming story about friendship, traditions, sports, and overcoming chronic illness, set in the Arctic. Inuit author Michael Arvaarluk Kusugak describes the arrival by propeller plane of six "standing-ups," or trees. Since no trees grow in the Arctic, the children don't know what they are. Eventually they carve the trees into baseball bats and spend long hours playing ball with children from a neighboring community. One child in the book, Arvaarluk, is asthmatic, yet he too enjoys hitting the ball and occasionally running the bases. Cultural traditions figure prominently in this book. At Christmas, each person chooses his favorite possession and gives it to his best friend. Arvaarluk's father gives away his only telescope and gets a wild dog in return.

Non-Native American and Canadian children are familiar with the game of baseball, so they understand the enjoyment the Inuit children in this book also derive from the game. This book goes a long way toward countering the goofy images of "Eskimos" that children are so often presented with. While baseball and friendships are similarities that are easy for children to grasp, children are also intrigued by the geographical and cultural differences described in this book. It is challenging for children to envision an environment where there are no trees and where teams of dogs pull sleds. Many children also find it hard to imagine giving away their most prized possession, even to their best friend. *Baseball Bats for Christmas* supplies powerful, positive images and much food for thought.

Writing—Giving Traditions

Baseball Bats for Christmas describes a giving tradition that is a part of Arvaarluk's culture. Teachers can introduce this activity by asking children to reflect on giving traditions in their own families. When are gifts given? Who does the giving? What types of gifts are given? Children can then write about these giving traditions and compare them with the traditions in Arvaarluk's community.

Reading—Toymaking

The children in *Baseball Bats for Christmas* are inventive in designing their own baseball bats. Other books explore how children use found objects to construct their own toys. A notable example is *Galimoto,* by Karen Lynn Williams, in which a child from Malawi builds his own toy car out of wire. Teachers can help children understand the similarities among groups of people by sharing these multicultural books that all relate to children's ability to make their own toys and games.

Art and Science—Creating Toys

After reading several books about children creating their own toys, children may wish to design toys of their own. Encourage children to think about what type of toy they would like to make. Children can make lists of inexpensive or free items they will need. They can then diagram how their toy will look. Finally, children can construct their toys and test them out. For example, the children in this photograph are making a dinosaur.

Not Recommended

1. Singling out children of various Nations (or tribes) for study

Sometimes teachers decide to "study" a particular Native American Nation. They might talk about this Nation's homes, clothes, children's games, and food. Such units generally position Native peoples somewhere in the past, living in wickiups, tipis, or longhouses while other people live in modern houses or apartment buildings. Even if the teacher tries to depict Native people today, setting them apart as a topic of study isolates them from the larger context of today's society and focuses more on differences than similarities. This is why we recommend talking about Native American peoples, and really all peoples, as part of all the general curricular units we already study.

2. Displaying pictures of children dressed up in stereotypical Native American attire, such as headdresses

Some teachers may harbor "cute" magazine photos in their picture files of children wrapped up in Indian blankets, wearing feathers, and huddled around a campfire. Such illustrations contribute to stereotypical images. Instead, teachers should seek out magazine photos of contemporary Native children to hang in our classrooms. Sally has discarded her offensive campfire picture and replaced it with a lovely photo of a Native American boy filling a bird feeder. The new picture was cropped from *National Geographic World*, a magazine for children.

3. Decorating teacher-made materials, such as charts or math games, with stereotypical stickers of children

Teachers interested in multicultural education may unwittingly contribute to stereotypes by illustrating class materials with what appear to be "adorable" stickers of children from around the world, but which actually perpetuate misconceptions and imbedded violent images. For example, a set of multicultural stickers from Hallmark depicts a "Sioux," or more appropriately, Lakota, child dressed in buckskins and headband, with tomahawk in hand. His hand is covering his mouth in the stereotypical "wah-wah" pose. The word "kola," which appears above the figure, is translated as hello, but actually means friend. A raised weapon and "war whoop" seem an unusual way to greet a friend. Other stickers in the set also convey stereotypes, but none of the children from other world cultures holds a weapon. In contrast, stickers of contemporary Native American leaders are available from Instructional Fair, Inc.

References

Eyvindson, Peter. 1994. *Kyle's bath*. Illustrated by Wendy Wolsak. Winnipeg: Pemmican Publications.

Harjo, Joy. 2000. *The good luck cat*. Illustrated by Paul Lee. San Diego: Harcourt.

Kusugak, Michael Arvaarluk. 1996. *Baseball bats for Christmas*. Art by Vladyana Krykorka. Toronto: Annick Press.

McClellan, Joe. 1995. *Nanabosho and the woodpecker*. Illustrated by Rhian Brynjolson. Winnipeg: Pemmican Publications.

Morris, Ann. 1995. *Shoes, shoes, shoes*. New York: Lothrop, Lee & Shepard.

Patrick, Denise Lewis. 1993. *Red dancing shoes*. Paintings by James E. Ransome. New York: Tambourine Books.

Sanderson, Esther. 1994. *Two pairs of shoes*. Illustrated by David Beyer. Winnipeg: Pemmican Publications.

Wheeler, Bernelda. 1992. *Where did you get your moccasins?* Illustrated by Herman Bekkering. Winnipeg: Peguis Publishers.

Williams, Karen Lynn. 1990. *Galimoto*. Illustrated by Catherine Stock. New York: Lothrop & Lee.

Wood, Audrey. 1985. *King Bidgood's in the bathtub*. Illustrated by Don Wood. San Diego: Harcourt Brace.

Chapter 3

Home Is Where the Heart Is

Guy's Perspective

I was at a Native American conference in November 2001, and I was amazed at the number of individuals there who gave different interpretations about the significance of the tipi. There is, of course, a spiritual interpretation as well as a physical interpretation. Everybody had a different story. The story that I relate to, and one that I think has special significance in today's times, was told to me by my grandma. When I asked her about the meaning of tipi, she said that the T at the beginning of "tipi" comes from the Lakota word chante *(pronounced tchahn-tay). (Chante starts with a "T" sound even though it is not spelled with a T when transliterated.) Chante is the heart, and tipi is the place of the heart. The poles of the tipi signify the ribcage of a person. Your ribs protect your heart, and that is what a tipi did. It protected the heart, because the heart of every community and every nation is the family. Tipi, then, is the place of the heart.*

I have noticed from watching my son Dakota that there are special places in our house where he goes when things are bothering him. Outside, under the trees, is a very personal place for him. He can feel the ground and his connectedness to it. He goes there when he's feeling hurt, and I leave him alone. I let him approach me when he's ready to talk.

The top of the washing machine is another one of his favorite spots. He says jiggling up and down on the top of the machine helps him stop thinking. For smaller problems, he will go into his bedroom and shut the door. There's no one fix-all place for him. Each of his special spots has its own soothing effect on him.

$ $ $

Sally's Perspective

One morning I stopped to chat with a grandmother who had just dropped her grandson off in his classroom. I knew she had been caring for him while his parents were out of town. "How's it going?" I asked. "Oh," she sighed. "I could not get Isaac up. He had the covers over his head and would not get out of the bed. He said Indians were creeping up the steps and were going to scalp him. I don't know where he gets this stuff. I'll be so glad when his mother gets home."

As teachers, we are often not aware of some of the fears that children harbor. On several occasions teachers have commented to me that they are sure the children in their classes don't have negative views of Native American people. Certainly Isaac's teacher had never heard him express fears or make derogatory comments about Indians. When incidents like this come up, it's all too easy to blame the family. In this case, the family was from a minority group themselves and very aware of multicultural issues. Families cannot shield their children from all the images in society. That's why teachers have an important role in countering those images.

Building on Similarities

The importance and meaning of the home, as described so eloquently in the Lakota language and traditions, connects children of all cultures. Children readily identify with photographs of homes from their own culture or community. Seeing reflections of their culture in the classroom helps children feel accepted and comfortable. Unfortunately, minority children, including many Native American children, often see little in the school environment that resembles their family or home. Guy has experienced this with his own son, as the following story describes.

Guy's Perspective

My son Dakota wants so much to be like his dad. He now knows why we wear our hair long, but there was a time when he was growing up when he wore his hair long just because his dad's hair was long. He didn't understand the tradition and meaning of the hair. Because he wore his hair long, he had to deal with children at school calling him "girl." Adults also referred to him as a "cute little girl," and gender misidentification became an issue. It got to the point where he was torn between being like his dad and cutting his hair. That was a struggle for him. He was too young to understand the spiritual aspects of the long hair, and I didn't expect him to. I would have let him cut his hair, but he still wanted it long like mine.

Dakota had been back to the reservation in South Dakota several times as a baby and young child, but he didn't remember it. Then, at age five, I took him back again. When we pulled up in front of my mom's house, all my nieces and nephews came running out. Dakota exclaimed delightedly, "Look! They're just like me." Then he understood. He became comfortable with himself when he saw other Indian children with their braided hair. Now he is no longer hurt by people's comments. He just laughs about it. Seeing other Indian children with long hair was vitally important to him. He had never seen images of contemporary Indian children in school.

Children naturally feel most comfortable when there are other children from their culture around them. When that is not possible, teachers should make every effort to have pictures and materials in the classroom that mirror the child's culture and ethnicity. For authentic cultural representations, teachers should consult with the child's family. This ensures that cultural or family traditions are not unknowingly misrepresented.

For example, one of the children in Sally's class a few years ago, Takuo, became much more comfortable in her classroom when he encountered pictures of buildings from his culture in the block area. Takuo's parents had come from Japan to pursue graduate degrees. Although Takuo spoke a little

English, his primary language was Japanese. The class had been in session for several months before he joined it, and most of the children already seemed to have special friends or play groups. Takuo looked around the classroom and then entered the block area. He carefully studied photographs of homes from around the world that were displayed in the area. Suddenly his face broke into a smile. Beckoning to one of the adults in the classroom, he pointed to a picture of a Japanese home and said, "That's me." Then he began to build with the blocks.

Appreciating Differences

Home is a special place for children, not because of the type of building, but because of the security, comfort, and love children find within. The importance of home is a unifying factor across cultures. As with other manifestations of culture, though, children typically first notice the differences among various types of homes, especially when the focus of the curriculum is on differences. For example, a hogan on the Diné (Navajo) reservation looks very different to urban children from an apartment building in New York. Without a focus on the meaning of home and the similarities among people, non-Native children may quickly come to regard Native peoples, as well as families from other cultures that they are not familiar with, as exotic, different, and probably inferior.

Teachers may unwittingly compound the problem. For example, some teachers try to teach about Indians by showing the types of homes various tribes, or Nations, historically used. This not only highlights differences rather than similarities, but also conveys the idea that American Indian people existed only in the past or live today as they did hundreds of years ago. Other teachers omit Native cultures when selecting pictures, books, or other curriculum materials for the classroom. This leaves non-Native children at the mercy of television and movies to educate them about Native peoples and leads many to conclude that all Indians live in tipis. Finally, some teachers fail to screen materials that they introduce into the classroom. An Indian block accessory that features tipis and canoes teaches misinformation because the toy combines materials from various Native cultures, as though all Indian peoples used the same homes, vehicles, and tools.

Books that depict Native peoples only in the past, even if written by Native American authors, also reinforce the misperceptions of non-Native children. Accurate representations of contemporary Native American people, homes, and businesses are essential if children are to understand American Indian people within the context of our world today. Once again we can turn to authentic Native American children's literature, written by acknowledged authors that represent their own cultures accurately, to help children clearly see the similarities among all people while also noticing cultural nuances.

Incorporating Native Perspectives into Curriculum

Homes and Toys

Chester Bear, Where Are You? by Peter Eyvindson, illustrated by Wendy Wolsak-Frith

Many parents and teachers have experienced the love young children have for books about beloved teddy bears. *Corduroy* and *Winnie the Pooh* come quickly to mind.

Here's another book in the heart-warming tradition of the lost teddy bear, but this time the story centers around a Native American child and his family. Kyle, the main character, has a special bear that accompanies him to school, on all of his play adventures, and most importantly, to bed each night. Then one day the bear is nowhere to be found. As Kyle searches for Chester Bear, we meet Kyle's computer-game-playing brothers, his newspaper-engrossed father, and his kind-hearted mother. Children quickly become immersed in the story because they, too, have special toys that periodically become lost. This commonality helps them readily identify with Kyle, the Native American child. The illustrations and text present a modern American Indian family, a strong counterimage to the "always in the past" stereotypes children typically see.

Children observe that Kyle's home is much like theirs, complete with television, toy box, bathroom, and bedroom. Subtle imagery, such as the pictures on the walls, conveys his Native roots.

Literacy—Teddy Bear Interactive Chart

Teachers often make literacy charts to coordinate with popular children's books. This chart has a four-line poem, printed on sentence strips, with spaces for two children to insert their names into the poem. The sentence strips are mounted on poster board along with an illustration of a teddy bear. Children can use magnetic tape to adhere their names to the chart.

Teddy Bear, Teddy Bear, he was lost.
Teddy Bear in the bedroom was tossed.
___(name)___ and ___(name)___ came and found,
Teddy Bear back, safe and sound.

Dramatic Play—Teddy Bears

Adding teddy bears to the dramatic play area gives children the opportunity to reenact popular books about teddy bears. *Chester Bear, Where Are You?* can be placed in the dramatic play area along with other books about teddy bears, such as *Corduroy,* by Don Freeman, *Ten Bears in My Bed,* by Stan Mack, and *When the Teddy Bears Came,* by Martin Waddell. Grouping books with multicultural characters around a common theme, such as teddy bears, helps children understand the similarities among peoples.

Writing—Lost Toys

Most children have misplaced or lost favorite toys. After reading *Chester Bear, Where Are You?*, children may wish to dictate or write their own stories about missing toys. They may want to bring a toy from home to write about. Teachers can compile the stories in a class book to share during group time or place on the bookshelf.

Writing Center— Chester Bear

Many preschool and kindergarten teachers include a writing center as part of their classrooms. The areas typically contain a variety of writing materials and interesting print models to provide a catalyst for writing. Writing centers that coordinate with favorite books help children link reading and writing. To build on children's interest in teddy bears and the book *Chester Bear, Where Are You?*, teachers might include word cards with the names of the characters in the book, sentence fill-in strips, and blank books shaped like teddy bears for children to write in.

Word Cards—Carefully print the names of the important characters in the book on 3 by 5-inch index cards, with one name per card. Illustrations of the characters can be included, if necessary, to help children read the words. Laminate the cards for durability. Words to incorporate might include Chester Bear, Kyle, Mommy, Daddy, and teddy bear. Additional words, such as Kristo, Konrad, and Toby, could be added later.

Sentence Fill-in Strips—Preprint the sentence below, leaving a blank space for children to fill in their own names, or the names of characters from the book, and what was lost. Children may want to write about their own experiences.

_____ *could not find* _____.

Teachers can print the sentence strips by hand or use a computer, set to a standard style of print, such as Arial. Several sentences can be written per page. They can be cut apart for display in the writing center.

Blank Books—Blank books, which can be cut in the shape of teddy bears, have front and back covers made of construction paper and several sheets of blank, inexpensive white paper inside. Children can use the blank books to copy word cards, write stories of their own, or dictate stories.

Math Game—Lost Bear

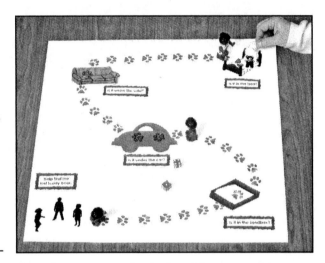

This math game, which coordinates with the theme of *Chester Bear, Where Are You?*, encourages children to construct numerical sets as they roll a die and advance their movers an equivalent number of spaces around the board. The game board, which is made of white poster board, 22 by 22 inches, features a bear-paw path made with a paw-print rubber stamp or stickers. Silhouette stickers of children mark the starting point for the movers, which are multicultural Duplo figures. Cut-outs of a sandbox, car, sofa, and bed illustrate places to look for a missing teddy bear.

The cut-outs, which are laminated and taped to the board, have toy stickers hidden beneath them. When players land on the space next to the cut-outs, they can lift them up to reveal lost toys. The last space on the game board is a pillow. When players reach the end and lift it up, they find a teddy bear sticker hidden beneath it.

This game links math with literacy. As children search for the missing teddy bear, they identify with Kyle and his lost bear. Older or more advanced children can roll two dice and add them together before moving along the path.

Homes and Nurturance

On Mother's Lap, by Ann Herbert Scott, illustrated by Glo Coalson

We often see grotesque caricatures of Inuit or other northern peoples, misnamed as Eskimos, in school curriculum.
Recently, Sally observed a phonics display in an elementary
school that showed two goofy people accompanied by the
phrase "Edgar and Edna, the energetic Eskimos." In contrast, *On Mother's Lap* tells a story of nurturing. A young
Native child, Michael, climbs onto his mother's lap to be
rocked, but repeatedly jumps down to bring more and
more toys to hold. Later, when his baby sister cries,
Michael tells his mother there's no more room on her
lap. Mother smiles, brings baby sister, and replies, "You
know, it's a funny thing, but there is always room on Mother's lap."

Many young children experience the addition of a baby to their families
and have to deal with the adjustments and conflicting emotions that arise.
Thus, all children can relate to the feelings explored in this charming book.
The illustrations are beautiful. Children see a Native child wrapped in the
love of his mother.

Literature—*Welcoming Babies*

Other children's books also explore the subject of a family's innate love for
their child. A notable example is *Welcoming Babies,* by Mary Burns Knight, with
illustrations by Anne Sibley O'Brien. The author describes the ways in which
various cultures welcome a new baby into the family. While each culture has
a different type of ceremony or tradition, all of the families demonstrate the
love and importance attached to the new child. Children see this similarity
clearly as they discuss this book.

Music—*The World Sings Goodnight*

Parents all over the world soothe their children to sleep by singing lullabies. The remarkable recording *The World Sings Goodnight* includes lullabies from thirty-three cultures, including Oglala Lakota, sung in their original languages. While children cannot understand the words of the many diverse languages, they can relate to the meaning and emotion of the music in much the same way that an infant, long before she can understand the meaning of the words her parent sings, feels soothed by the melody and falls asleep. The recording gives children the opportunity to hear the cadence of diverse languages. In multilingual classrooms, children may become very excited when they hear a song in their own language.

Writing—Special Places

I like the big tree by my house. There's a squirrel that lives there.

Earlier, we heard about Dakota's special places in his home. Many children have a special place that they retreat to for comfort, security, quiet play, or daydreaming. It might be their bed or bedroom, the front porch, a rocking chair, or under the dining room table. For this activity, children can think about where that special place is for them. They can dictate their thoughts to an adult or write their ideas themselves. Children may enjoy sharing their ideas with their friends, or they may prefer to keep them private, perhaps as part of a journal.

Dramatic Play—Babies

The dramatic play area gives children the opportunity to explore, through play, a variety of roles and emotions. Playing with multicultural dolls, including Native American dolls, encourages children to nurture infants and take on the role of father or mother. Since most cultures have devised ways to safely carry infants, whether in backpacks, cloth slings, or cradleboards, including a variety of baby carriers in the dramatic play area allows children to experience the similarities among cultures (all carry their babies), as well

as the differences. If baby carriers are not available, children can compare photographs of them displayed in the area or look at illustrations in books. Seeing photos of American Indian fathers cuddling their children is a strong counterimage to the tomahawk-carrying warrior that is so often portrayed. In one classroom, parents from various cultures were invited to visit and demonstrate baby carriers from their Nations. Teachers can also include various types of blankets, soothing music, and perhaps a rocking chair in the area.

Homes and Creativity

Abuela's Weave, by Omar S. Castañeda, illustrated by Enrique O. Sánchez

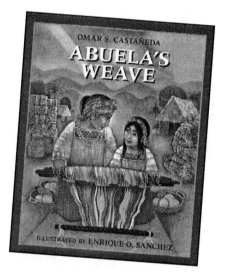

Many families have cultural or personal art traditions that are carried out in the home. In *Abuela's Weave,* we meet a young Mayan girl and her grandmother who live in a village in Guatemala. They are Native people from Central America who still carry on the traditional art of weaving. Esperanza, the young girl in the story, worries that no one will buy the weavings that she and Abuela, her grandmother, create since so much cloth is now produced in factories. An additional concern is her grandmother's birthmark, which frightens some people and drives them away. As Abuela and Esperanza travel to the city, we notice many aspects of their culture, including villages, baskets, marketplaces, and artwork containing traditional symbols. We also see that they live in today's world, with buses and honking cars in the city. Although North American children can quickly tell that Esperanza comes from a culture different from theirs, they readily identify with her close relationship with her grandmother, the difficulties they face, and the beautiful weavings they create together. After hearing this book, many children relate stories of quilts or afghans their own mothers or grandmothers have made.

Literature—Quilt Books

A number of excellent children's books explore quilt and sewing traditions in a variety of cultures. The unifying factors among all of these books are the close family relationships, the use of fabrics to create artwork, and the incorporation of symbols or designs that have special meaning to particular cultures. The following list may provide a starting point in assembling books about quilting and sewing traditions.

The Quilt, by Ann Jonas—African American tradition
Sweet Clara and the Keeping Quilt, by Deborah Hopkinson—African American tradition
The Keeping Quilt, by Patricia Polacco—Jewish tradition
Luka's Quilt, by Georgia Guback—Hawaiian tradition
The Patchwork Quilt, by Valerie Flournoy—African American tradition
The Quilt Story, by Tony Johnston—pioneer tradition
Something from Nothing, by Phoebe Gilman—Jewish tradition
Charlie Needs a Cloak, by Tomie dePaola—weaving process

Art—Class Quilts

After reading *Abuela's Weave* and other books about quilting and weaving traditions, children are excited to create their own class quilt. A sampler quilt allows children to sew designs on pieces of colorful burlap, approximately 7 inches square, using large plastic needles and colorful yarn. The burlap can be mounted on small embroidery hoops to keep it from bunching up as children sew. Some children like to make designs with their stitches or sew symbols that have special meaning for them onto their burlap. Other decorative items can be added to the squares, such as beads with large holes, pieces of lace, or colorful spangles. Once each child has completed a square, the pieces can be sewed together to create a class quilt and displayed in the school. Class quilts allow children to explore their own cultures and creativity while combining their efforts to create a group project.

Teachers might also wish to make family quilts with their classes. Felt provides a good medium for decorative quilts because families can sew, draw, or glue items to the felt, whatever method suits them. Teachers can send a square of felt home with each child along with information about the family quilt, or families can assemble at the school for a celebration and make their quilt squares at that time. Through letters sent home or informal conversations with the teachers, families are encouraged to include aspects of their cultural or family traditions on their quilt squares. Children love to describe the square their family has made and relate what each

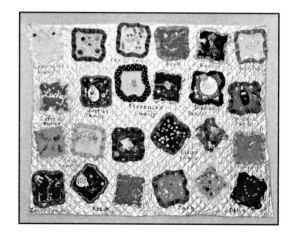

design or object represents. Family quilts draw the class together as they work on a community project, while preserving and valuing the individual aspects of each child's family and culture. In a family quilt created by one of Sally's classes, a family with Native ancestry included Ojibway beadwork on their square. A family from Cambodia wrote in their native language on the quilt, and a family with African ancestry included African trade beads and cloth on their square.

Art—Display Quilts or Fabric

Willow Ann Soltow (1991, xii) writes, "Historically, throughout the world, women's needlework has been regarded as a documentation of life's activities. Every stitch taken in a creative spirit is an answer to despair; every knotted thread an affirmation of peaceful human endeavor." Teachers can help children appreciate the beauty of quilts, fabrics, and weavings from various cultures by displaying samples in the classroom. While actual examples are always preferable, photographs can certainly substitute. Calendars are a good source of quilt pictures, and families may have actual examples of fabric or quilts to share. Native American examples could include star quilts from the Lakota tradition, *arpilleras* (appliquéd figures and scenes) from the Native peoples of the

Andes, Seminole patchwork, Diné (Navajo) weavings, and *molas* (appliquéd panels) from the Cuna people of what is now Panama.

Homes and Food

The Story of the Milky Way, by Joseph Bruchac and Gayle Ross, with paintings by Virginia A. Stroud

The Story of the Milky Way, by Joseph Bruchac (Abenaki) and Gayle Ross (Cherokee), is a traditional Cherokee story that depicts the importance of corn to the people. The book begins in today's time, with a father or grandfather telling the story to his children. Then the traditional tale of the missing cornmeal begins, complete with a mystery that a young boy helps to solve. The illustrations, by Cherokee artist Virginia A. Stroud, are stunning.

Cooking—Popcorn

All corn, including popcorn, comes from the Native peoples of the Americas. An exciting way to explore corn is through cooking popcorn. While many children have eaten popcorn, most have not seen it on the cob.

Teachers can find popcorn on the cob in some health food stores or grocery stores. Children can pluck the kernels from the cob before popping it in a pan or popcorn popper. (Teachers will, of course, need to handle the popping part of the activity for safety.)

After popping popcorn, many children also want to try to pop regular corn on the cob. Teachers can place a few kernels of corn in a pan over heat so children can see that it doesn't pop. The corn can then be cooked in water and eaten. Children can compare the difference between the two types of corn.

Science—Grinding Corn

Corn has become such an important food staple around the world that many are unaware that domestic corn originated with the Native people of the Americas, who cultivated many varieties to suit various needs and growing conditions. Typically, we label multicolored corn as "Indian corn," but it is more accurate to inform children that all corn is Indian corn.

Children can explore the change in form that occurs when dried corn is pounded into a powder. Use of a traditional mortar and pestle gives children hands-on experience with the process. A mortar is a deep bowl made of wood or marble, and a pestle is a rounded dowel used for pounding. Children can grind various types of corn and compare the resulting cornmeal. Is all cornmeal white? Is the powder from ground corn the same color as the original corn? These are questions children can answer through experimenting with the corn. Later, children can cook with packaged cornmeal, and perhaps make muffins or cornbread.

Not Recommended

1. Putting a tipi in the classroom

Child-size tipis are commercially available, but we do not recommend including them in the classroom because they reinforce children's misconceptions that all Indian peoples lived in tipis and that they still do today. In addition, materials like tipis and forts seem to stimulate cowboy and Indian play, a violent play theme teachers should avoid.

2. Dress-up clothes with Indian sports mascots

Teachers need to be on the lookout for offending images that perpetuate the very stereotypes we hope to counter in the classroom. Since many athletic teams use Indians as mascots, we have to scrutinize sports-related apparel that might be used for dramatic play. For example, a ball cap with

Chief Wahoo of the Cleveland Indians, called a "red Sambo" by many Native American people, would not be an appropriate addition to the classroom. Teachers should, of course, guard against stereotypes of any race or culture.

3. Food containers with stereotypical images

Stereotypes can also slip into our classrooms on food containers that we might use as dramatic play props. Sometimes we are so used to seeing these images that we fail to notice the stereotypes they contain. For example, Land o' Lakes butter has an image that appears to be an Indian princess on the container. There were no Indian princesses. Early settlers sometimes imparted royal designations to Native leaders because they had come from monarchies themselves; however, Native peoples are quick to clarify that they never had kings, queens, princes, or princesses. When we bring materials into the classroom that portray such images, we are supplying misinformation and perpetuating stereotypes.

Calumet baking powder is another food container with a stereotypical logo, in this case, the noble warrior in full headdress. In years past, teachers had to scrutinize food containers for images such as Aunt Jemima. We must remain on watch today.

References

Bruchac, Joseph, and Gayle Ross. 1995. *The story of the Milky Way.* Paintings by Virginia A. Stroud. New York: Dial Books.

Castañeda, Omar S. 1993. *Abuela's weave.* Illustrated by Enrique O. Sánchez. New York: Lee & Low.

dePaola, Tomie. 1988. *Charlie needs a cloak.* New York: Simon and Schuster Books for Young Readers.

Eyvindson, Peter. 1988. *Chester bear, where are you?* Illustrated by Wendy Wolsak-Frith. Winnipeg: Pemmican Publications.

Flournoy, Valerie. 1985. *The patchwork quilt.* Pictures by Jerry Pinkney. New York: Dial.

Freeman, Don. 1968. *Corduroy.* New York: Viking Press.

Gilman, Phoebe. 1992. *Something from nothing.* New York: Scholastic.

Guback, Georgia. 1994. *Luka's quilt.* New York: Greenwillow.

Hopkinson, Deborah. 1993. *Sweet Clara and the keeping quilt.* Illustrated by James Ransome. New York: Knopf.

Johnston, Tony. 1985. *The quilt story.* Pictures by Tomie de Paola. New York: Scholastic.

Jonas, Ann. 1984. *The quilt.* New York: Greenwillow.

Knight, Mary Burns. 1994. *Welcoming babies.* Illustrations by Anne Sibley O'Brien. Gardiner, Maine: Tilbury House.

Mack, Stan. 1974. *Ten bears in my bed.* New York: Pantheon Books.

Polacco, Patricia. 1988. *The keeping quilt.* New York: Simon & Schuster.

Scott, Ann Herbert. 1993. *On mother's lap.* Illustrated by Glo Coalson. New York: Scholastic.

Soltow, Willow Ann. 1991. *Quilting the world over.* Radnor, Pa.: Chilton Book Company.

Waddell, Martin. 1994. *When the teddy bears came.* Illustrated by Penny Dale. Cambridge, Mass.: Candlewick Press.

The world sings goodnight. 1993. Boulder, Colo.: Silverwave Records SC–803.

Chapter 4

Families—The Importance of Relatives

Guy's Perspective

Family structures in many traditional Native American cultures differ from the nuclear family organization in many American homes. Grandparents, aunts, and uncles are all integral parts of the family. In my Lakota upbringing, the main responsibility of parents was to love and provide sustenance for their children. Grandparents, aunts, and uncles took the important roles of teachers and disciplinarians. This does not mean that parents did not also teach and provide discipline, but primarily they gave unconditional love and support while grandparents, aunts, and uncles concerned themselves with teaching and guidance. In the Lakota culture, aunties are also considered to be a child's mothers, and uncles are their fathers.

Sometimes high school students ask me how many wives I have. They have trouble understanding the differences in family structures. In terms of mainstream culture, I am married and have a wife. In Lakota society, on the other hand, I have a partner who completes me and is called my "half-side." We have children together. Her sisters are considered to be my wives because my responsibility is to teach and discipline her sisters' children. I am called "grandfather" by the children of my nieces and nephews. This closely aligned family structure does not mean, though, that Lakota men have more than one partner, or half-side.

When schools call the family of a Native American child to come to school for a conference, they should not be surprised if an uncle, aunt, or grandparent also comes. That is their role. If the school tries to exclude this important family member, it can create a barrier between the school and the family. Schools should let families decide who needs to be at the conference and thus foster cooperation and support between home and school.

Educators should also realize that not all Native American families are part of traditional, extended families. Many have assimilated into mainstream society and have family structures and roles that are similar to the dominant culture. Schools cannot make assumptions about any child's family structure. That is why it is so important for teachers to get to know the families of the children they teach.

$ $ $

Sally's Perspective

The dramatic play area of our classroom had been transformed into a dance area, complete with dance attire and multicultural shoes. Children could watch themselves in a large mirror as they danced to an international selection of music. In order to help children draw the connection between dance and its representation in diverse cultures, pictures of dancers from around the world were also displayed in the area. Donte entered the dance center and looked at all of the pictures. He examined photos of dancers from Africa, Cambodia, and Hawaii without commenting. Then he saw a poster of two Native American dancers, in colorful regalia, leaping into the air. "Those men are bad!" Donte exclaimed. "Indians are bad. They'll kill you. They'll scalp you."

Momentarily at a loss for words, I recovered and reassured Donte that they were dancers. I had met them during a festival, and I remarked that they were very pleasant people, and also quite talented. Donte remained unconvinced, and I realized that he had already formed frightening impressions of American Indian people. In order to counter those ideas, I invited a Diné (Navajo) friend to visit the classroom. I asked him to come and just "hang out" so the children could get to know him.

Joseph arrived with his two-year-old son as the children were engaged in free-choice activities. He wore jeans and a shirt, lizard boots, and a beautiful turquoise necklace. With his long black hair and dark complexion, the children immediately identified him as Native American. As I went to greet Joseph, Donte hid behind my dress, clinging to *it. He seemed very frightened but also curious. Joseph knelt down and began to show the children his necklace. Meanwhile, his son raced around the room looking at the class pets and examining the toys. Gradually Donte emerged from behind my back and also began looking at the necklace.*

During the course of the afternoon, the children enjoyed many interchanges with Joseph. With playdough and a wooden hammer, he showed them how he could tap out designs in silver such as those on his necklace. Then several children asked Joseph if he lived in a tipi. Taking paper and markers, he drew a picture of his house in Dayton— definitely not a tipi! Then he asked them to draw pictures of their homes for him. When snacks arrived, several children invited Joseph to join them at the table. As he began sipping his juice, the children asked in amazement, "Do you like apple juice?" "Yes," he replied. "Do you?"

At first, Donte watched Joseph from a distance. Gradually, he got closer and closer until he joined Joseph's group at the snack table. When it was time for Joseph to gather up his son and leave, Donte asked him if he could come back. He had now formed a new image of Native American people, an image of kindness, caring, and nurturing.

Building on Similarities

Not every classroom has the opportunity to have a special visitor like Joseph to help dispel fears and myths, but all classrooms can celebrate the similarities among peoples through carefully selected literature and curriculum materials. Unfortunately, in many cases the only images children see of Native peoples are violent ones. The stories they hear are of marauding Indians attacking peaceful pioneers. At an educator's conference on the Oneida reservation in Wisconsin, conference organizer Brian Doxtater commented, "Why are warrior images the only ones people ever have of us? Why don't they ever see us as fathers and husbands and teachers and doctors?" This is a question all educators must take to heart, including those of us working with the youngest children.

Talking about families gives us many opportunities to focus on our commonalities as people. As we share multicultural books about families in our classrooms, children quickly perceive that children from other races and cultures also have families that love and nurture them. Reading about Native families of today, looking at lovely illustrations or photographs, and participating in curriculum extensions of books by Native American authors help children counter imbedded stereotypes and focus on likenesses instead.

Appreciating Differences

Of course not all families are the same, even within a particular culture or race of people. Helping children understand and appreciate differences in family structures is also part of our responsibility as educators. For example, not all families have a mommy and a daddy. Some children are raised by a single parent, a grandparent, a foster family, an aunt or uncle, or two mommies or daddies. As discussed earlier, traditional Native American families may have aunts, uncles, and grandparents fulfilling important child-rearing roles. Families also have different traditions. Some go to powwows, while others go camping or visit the beach each summer. As children discover the special qualities of families, they can reflect on their own families and their unique experiences.

Incorporating Native American Perspectives into Curriculum

Families and Traditions

Jingle Dancer, by Cynthia Leitich Smith, illustrated by Cornelius Van Wright and Ying-Hwa Hu

Jingle Dancer, by Muscogee author Cynthia Leitich Smith, introduces children to a young Muscogee (Creek) girl, Jenna, who longs to carry on the tradition of jingle dancing that has been shared by generations of women in her family. Her problem is how to acquire enough jingles, the cone-shaped tin or aluminum lids that clink together during dancing, for her dress. Jenna hits upon a plan. She begins to ask each of her female relatives for a few of their jingles so that they will retain enough jingles for their dresses, but she will be able to make a jingle dress of her own. As Jenna talks to her extended family, we meet Great-aunt Sis, who tells traditional stories; Mrs. Scott, who is making fry bread; Cousin Elizabeth, who is an attorney; and Grandma Wolfe, who jingle dances on video. Jenna is a contemporary child who turns to her family and community for help. She is honored by her role in her family and eager to carry on family and cultural traditions. The children we teach understand family values, such as respect and love, from their own experiences. This book gives them a chance to see a nurturing Native American family of today as well as some of the unique aspects of their culture.

Literature—Dance Books

Many cultures have their own special dance traditions. By introducing children to a variety of children's books based on dance, teachers can help them not only recognize dance as a thread that travels through many cultures, but also explore the unique aspects of each culture's dance traditions. The following suggested books could be incorporated into classroom dance centers or reading areas.

Mimi's Tutu, by Tynia Thomassie—African American
Silent Lotus, by Jeanne M. Lee—Cambodian
Lion Dancer, by Kate Waters and Madeline Slovenz-Low—Chinese American
Powwow, by George Ancona—Native American
Color Dance, by Ann Jonas—multiracial
Red Dancing Shoes, by Denise Lewis Patrick—African American
My Ballet Class, by Rachel Isadora—multiracial
Song and Dance Man, by Karen Ackerman—multigenerational
Lili on Stage, by Rachel Isadora—multiracial

Dramatic Play and Movement—Dance Area

Children enjoy experiencing dancing firsthand through their own body movements. A dance area in the classroom gives children the opportunity to express themselves through dance. In order to help children recognize that dance is important in many cultures, teachers can play music from many nationalities. However, when including music from Native American cultures, teachers must be highly selective. Much Native music is intended for sacred or ceremonial use by people who are aware of its cultural significance; therefore, most powwow music would not be appropriate for a class dance area. One recording we can recommend is *Kids' Pow-Wow Songs,* recorded by the Black Lodge Singers. It includes twelve playful songs for children of all ages to dance to.

Teachers may also wish to add a variety of dance outfits for both boys and girls to the dance area. Dress-ups might include the following:

lapas—African skirts, made by wrapping a yard of African fabric around the waist and tying

colorful vests, easily made from felt

tutus—traditional European ballet attire, which can be made from stretch halters sewed to several layers of netting

small kimonos—wide-sleeved robes from Japan

silky shirts

tap shoes

moccasins

fancy sandals or slippers

While it is appropriate to display pictures of Native American dancers in the area, along with dancers from a variety of nationalities, teachers should avoid including feathers, which are considered sacred in most Native cultures, and traditional Native American dance regalia. For Native peoples, dance regalia convey sacred and cultural meanings that cannot be equated with a dance costume or dress-up clothes.

Writing Center—Dancers

Children interested in dancing may also be inspired to write about their experiences. Teachers can design a class writing center to coordinate with a dance theme. The area might include word cards with the names of dance items, pencils decorated with stickers of dance shoes, and blank books shaped like dance shoes.

Word Cards—Carefully print the name of each dance item on a separate 3 by 5-inch index card. Illustrate each word card with a sticker or drawing of the item to help children read the words. Laminate the cards for durability. Words to incorporate might include *moccasins, jingle dress, lapa, tutu,* and *vest.*

Fancy Pencils—Fancy pencils often inspire children to write. Dance-theme pencils can be easily made by adhering dance-shoe stickers to sparkly pencils.

Blank Books—Blank books shaped like moccasins or ballet shoes encourage children to copy word cards, experiment with writing, or dictate dance stories. Moccasin books can be made with brown construction paper for the front and back covers and several pieces of inexpensive white paper inside. Ballet-shoe books might have colored paper on the front and back and white paper inside.

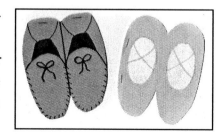

Music—Dance Video

It would be wonderful for classes to attend a real powwow, with music, dancing, food, art works, storytelling, and interesting people. Check around your area to see if any are scheduled. If attending a powwow is not possible, teachers may consider showing clips from a powwow videotape recording, such as *Into the Circle*. (Individuals who wish to videotape a powwow should be aware that certain dances or ceremonial portions of powwows may not be photographed or videotaped. The announcer will usually inform the public when cameras are not allowed.) A powwow dancing video segment might be introduced along with other video clips showing various types of dancing from around the world, with perhaps one type viewed briefly and discussed each day. Since young children would typically rather be moving around than watching others dance, viewing time should be limited, perhaps to between five and ten minutes.

Even such a short viewing can have a dramatic effect on children's attitudes. For example, Sally selected one section of the video to show her preschool class. After reviewing the entire tape recording, she chose a portion that highlighted a young fancy dancer because it contained lots of activity, color, and excitement. When the children first saw the dancer on the television screen, several remarked that they didn't like him.

"I think he's bad," declared a young girl.

"Let's listen to what he says," Sally replied.

The dancer was then interviewed on the video. He talked about what dancing meant to him, how hard he had worked to learn the dance traditions and become skilled at moving correctly, and how much he hoped he would win the dance competition at the powwow. When the dancing started, the children all began to root for him. They seemed to have been moved by his quiet voice and sincerity. When he did, in fact, win the competition, the children cheered loudly.

Into the Circle also contains a section on jingle dancing. Teachers who incorporate the book *Jingle Dancer* into their curriculum might wish to show that portion of the video.

Families through the Seasons

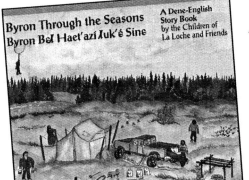

Byron Through the Seasons,
by the Children of La Loche and Friends

Teachers often highlight the seasons of the year with young children as they unfold. They might introduce books related to seasons and incorporate natural materials related to a particular time of the year into science areas. Families also often have special activities or traditions that are seasonal. *Byron Through the Seasons* describes how Dene families in Canada enjoy the seasons at their camp on the bay. The book was written and illustrated by children from Ducharme Elementary School in La Loche, Saskatchewan, with assistance from local advisors and elders. It is written in both English and the Dene language. Children learn about many cultural traditions as they listen to the story: catching and preparing fish, making and decorating moccasins, cutting ice blocks to preserve fish in summer, tanning hides, gardening, and picking medicinal plants. They also notice many activities that are similar to things they may do with their families, such as cooking outside, camping out in tents, playing in the snow, and gardening. *Byron Through the Seasons* shows Native children and families of today. Although long-standing traditions are still followed, modern accoutrements, such as pickup trucks, schoolhouses, and snowmobiles, are also present.

Writing—Our Families through the Seasons

After reading *Byron Through the Seasons* and other books about families and their traditions, children may wish to write about their own families and the things they do together at various times of the year. Children can write or dictate their stories and then illustrate them. One class displayed their stories in the hallway outside their classroom. They often stopped to read them on their way to and from class. Other children also stopped to look at the stories and often asked to have them read.

Teachers might wish to reintroduce this activity each time the seasons change. Each child's stories could be compiled into a book to send home at the end of the year. Activities such as this help children bond as a group. They notice the similarities among family activities and also aspects that are unique to their own culture or experiences.

Dramatic Play—Campground

Byron Through the Seasons describes a community's activities throughout the year that revolve around a campground. Many children have had similar camping experiences, whether on an overnight stay in a park, in a friend's backyard, or on an actual camping trip with their family. For this reason, teachers might incorporate a campground into their dramatic play or outside areas.  Small tents, perhaps made by draping a bedspread over an A-frame; small grills (not to be lit!); flannel shirts; and outdoor cooking equipment could be included.

Writing Center—Family Seasonal Traditions

Children may wish to continue writing about camping or seasonal family activities after they have written family stories as a special activity. Relevant materials can be incorporated into a class writing center.

snowflake

Word Cards—Decide which word cards are important to include for your class. Examples might be camping items, if there is a campground in the classroom, or seasonal words, such as *winter, snow, autumn, leaves, summer, swim, spring,* and *garden*. Carefully print each word on a separate 3 by 5-inch index card. Illustrate each word card with a sticker or drawing to help children read the words. Laminate the cards for durability.

Fill-in Strips—Early writers can be more independent if key phrases are already written for them. For this center, teachers might include the following fill-in strip:

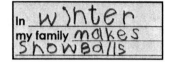

In _____, my family _____.

Children can fill in the first blank space with a season and the second space with what their family likes to do. Teachers can print the fill-in strips by hand or use a word-processing program set to a font that looks like standard print. Include multiple copies of the fill-in strips in the center.

Seasonal Blank Books—Interesting blank books related to seasons are easy to make. Inexpensive notepads with shapes that correlate with the seasons are available in teacher supply stores and catalogs, office supply stores, and stationery stores. One sheet of paper from a notepad can serve as the cover of each blank book, so typically fifty covers can be made from one notepad. Interior paper can be cut in the same shape as the cover from free or inexpensive paper. Shapes available include leaves for autumn, snowpeople for winter, flowers for spring, and seashells for summer. Children can use the blank books for writing stories, copying words, or drawing.

Families and Self-Awareness

Less Than Half, More Than Whole,
by Kathleen and Michael Lacapa

Many of the children that we teach today come from families of more than one race or culture. Census figures suggest that this will increasingly be the case. Sometimes children who are biracial or multiracial feel left out or rejected by other children. They may think that they don't fit into either culture. *Less Than Half, More Than Whole,* by authors Kathleen Lacapa (Irish, English, and Mohawk) and Michael Lacapa (Apache, Hopi, and Tewa) deals with this issue in a sensitive way through the loving intervention of a child's grandfather. The story begins with three friends looking at their reflections in a lake. The boys notice that one is blond with light-colored skin, another has brown skin and black hair, and the third, Tony, is somewhere in between. "You're not like me," his friend Will tells him. "I'm all Indian. I think you're only half, or less than half." This comment causes Tony to question who he really is. He is helped by his grandfather, who shows him photographs of all the members of their extended family and points out how different and special each one is. The illustrations in *Less Than Half, More Than Whole* are filled with beautiful colors and Native imagery. Southwestern Native culture is accurately depicted throughout the book. The authors, who represent mixed Native and Anglo heritage themselves, work with children in and around the White Mountain Apache Reservation.

Literature—Books about Families

Less Than Half, More Than Whole explores the emotions of a child who is of mixed Native American and Caucasian descent. Other books show a variety of types of families. A notable example is *Foster Baby,* written and illustrated by Rhian Brynjolson, which sensitively describes a Native American baby in a loving Native foster home. Teachers may wish to introduce books from the selection listed below to help children understand similarities and differences among families.

Black Is Brown Is Tan, by Arnold Adoff—family with a Caucasian father and an African American mother

More, More, More Said the Baby, by Vera B. Williams—Caucasian baby and father; Asian baby and mother; African American baby and Caucasian grandmother

The Mommy Book, by Ann Morris—mothers and children from around the world

The Daddy Book, by Ann Morris—fathers and children from around the world

The Village of Round and Square Houses, by Ann Grifalconi—West African family

Aunt Flossie's Hats, by Elizabeth Fitzgerald Howard—African American extended family

Best Best Colors, by Eric Hoffman—child with two mothers

Mama Zooms, by Jane Cowen-Fletcher—child has a mother in a wheelchair

Art—Self-Portraits

Art is a natural vehicle for children to explore skin and hair colors and tones. Children can look into small cosmetic mirrors as they draw their own portraits. Teachers can facilitate by providing markers, crayons, or paint in multi-cultural skin tones. They can help children mix colors to match their skin or hair color, if desired by the child. Of course, teachers should allow children to draw themselves as they choose. Deciding to paint blue hair, perhaps because that is a child's favorite color, is perfectly acceptable from a creative standpoint. Sally can recall observing in a kindergarten class where children were drawing people. A little girl was reprimanded for drawing a woman with orange hair. "People don't have orange hair," the teacher declared. Looking at a strand of her light auburn hair (read "orange"), Sally could only wonder about the comment.

Family Participation—Family Diaries

Family diaries, an activity designed by Monica Battle at the Arlitt Child and Family Research and Education Center,

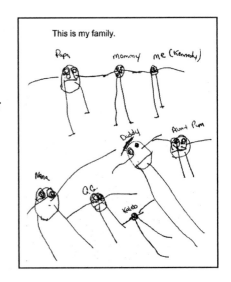

This is my family.

Papa   mommy   me (Kennedy)

Daddy   Aunt Pam

Nana   G.G.   Koceo

University of Cincinnati, are a collaborative effort of parents and teachers. They serve as an important link between home and school for children. At the beginning of the year, each family contributes several pages for their child's diary. Examples include a photograph of the child and other family members, a letter to the child describing their special traits and interests, and a description of what the child and family have done over the summer. As the year progresses, teachers add pages to each child's diary that depict special activities in the classroom. Examples of children's art and writing creations can also be included. Children can look at their family diaries and share them with one another whenever they wish.

For the parents of Kennedy
Please send a message to your child that will be a permanent part of their diary. It can be a phrase, a letter, a photo, or a memento.

Kennedy,
I am so proud of you helping out and being the big sister. You help me feed him, change him and help with baths. You are my helper, thanks Kennedy ☺
Mommy

Kennedy,
You are a wonderful daughter. You are full of love, life, and joy. Never compromise who you are. Always pursue your passion, that thing that makes you truly happy. I am so happy to have you in my life.
— Daddy Man
P.S. I absolutely love your smile!
Keep smiling!

Families and Loss

Fox Song, by Joseph Bruchac, illustrated by Paul Morin

Unfortunately, most children have to deal with the loss of a loved one at one time or another. This could involve the death of a parent, sibling, grandparent, or even a pet. *Fox Song,* by the noted Abenaki author Joseph Bruchac, tells the story of a young Abenaki girl, Jamie, whose grandmother has died. Jamie eases her sadness with recollections of the many special times she spent with her grandmother: picking blackberries, harvesting birch bark for baskets, tasting sap from the maple tree, and watching the falling leaves. Grandmother tells Jamie, "We say that those that have gone are no further away from us than the leaves that have fallen." She shows Jamie the tracks of Wokwses, the Fox, and tells her, "When you are out here and I am not with you, you keep your eyes open. You might see her, and when you do, you will think of me." Then she teaches Jamie a special song. Following the death of her grandmother, Jamie walks through the forest and soon sees a fox. She sings the special song taught to her by her grandmother and knows she will never be alone.

Fox Song is beautifully written and illustrated. Cultural traditions are readily apparent in the teachings of the grandmother and the activities she shares with Jamie. The love between grandmother and granddaughter transcends culture and is something all children can understand and identify with.

Literature—Related Books

Other children's authors also deal sensitively with the topic of death. One notable example is from Inuit author Michael Arvaarluk Kusugak, *Northern Lights: The Soccer Trails*. We meet a young Inuit girl, Kataujaq, and learn of her close relationship with her mother. They travel on sea ice in a canoe pulled by dogs, pick berries, and sing traditional songs together. Kataujaq loves to collect flowers and stones for her mother, who carefully saves and preserves all of them. Then a sickness comes and Kataujaq loses her mother. She is very sad. One night she watches as her village plays soccer under the stars and northern lights. Her grandmother tells her that the lights are the souls of loved ones who have died, and they are playing soccer up in the sky. As Kataujaq watches the aurora borealis, she feels close to her mother and is comforted.

This book won the Ruth Schwartz Award from the Ontario Arts Council and Canadian Booksellers Association. Children are entranced by the breathtaking illustrations and surprised to learn that the Inuit, people they had always called "Eskimos," also play soccer, a familiar game to all of them.

Not Recommended

1. Native American dance regalia in dramatic play

As previously indicated, traditional Native American dance regalia should not be equated with a dance costume. The regalia of Native dancers represent a part of their personal identity and also their affiliation with a particular Indian Nation. Since regalia are considered sacred, it is very inappropriate to include it in a classroom dance area.

2. Asking children to make up stories about a fictitious Indian family

Children cannot make up stories about families from cultures they don't know. None of us can. When we urge non-Native children to create fictitious Indian families, we force them to rely on inaccuracies and stereotypes, thereby reinforcing the very misconceptions we hope to counter. In a classroom recently visited by Guy, children were given just such an assignment. They were asked to "describe your Indian and what *it* wears." Needless to say, terminology such as this, coupled with the nature of the assignment, demeans and objectifies American Indian peoples. Instead, teachers can ask children to write about their own families. They can also read stories to the class about Native families written by Native authors.

3. Asking children to invent "Indian myths"

In the book *Northern Lights: The Soccer Trails,* author Michael Arvaarluk Kusugak shares a traditional spiritual belief of his people. In school and in the dominant culture, we tend to label the deeply held beliefs and stories of other peoples as myths. While books about more dominant religions, such as Christian, Hindu, Jewish, and Muslim, appear under a *religions* category in the school library, the religious beliefs of indigenous people, notably American Indians, are categorized as myths. This denigrates both their religion and them as people. Worse yet is an activity that asks children to make up Indian myths, which Guy and Sally noticed in a literacy activity book, *Art and Writing throughout the Year* (Walrows and Tekerean 1989), for sale at the 2000 NAEYC (National Association for the Education of Young Children) national conference. Teachers must remember that a culture's traditional stories have been handed down for timeless generations. They are not made up by contemporary people. In addition, traditional stories often have deep spiritual meaning and are no different from Bible stories to Christian or Jewish children, or stories from the Koran to Muslim children. We would never ask children to make up their own Bible stories, and we should never ask them to make up "myths" from other cultures.

References

Ackerman, Karen. 1988. *Song and dance man.* Illustrated by Stephen Gammell. New York: Knopf.

Adoff, Arnold. 1973. *Black is brown is tan.* Pictures by Emily Arnold McCully. New York: Harper & Row.

Ancona, George. 1993. *Powwow.* New York: Harcourt.

Black Lodge Singers, performers. 1996. *Kids' pow-wow songs.* Phoenix, Ariz.: Canyon Records, CR–6274, vol. 14.

Bruchac, Joseph. 1993. *Fox song.* Illustrated by Paul Morin. New York: Philomel Books.

Brynjolson, Rhian. 1996. *Foster baby.* Winnipeg: Pemmican Publications.

Children of La Loche and Friends. 1990. *Byron through the seasons.* Saskatoon: Fifth House Publishers.

Cowen-Fletcher, Jane. 1993. *Mama zooms.* New York: Scholastic.

Grifalconi, Ann. 1986. *The village of round and square houses.* Boston: Little, Brown.

Hoffman, Eric. 1999. *Best best colors.* Illustrated by Celeste Henriquez. St. Paul: Redleaf Press.

Howard, Elizabeth Fitzgerald. 1991. *Aunt Flossie's hats.* Paintings by James Ransome. New York: Clarion.

Into the circle. 1992. Tulsa: Full Circle Communications.

Isadora, Rachel. 1980. *My ballet class.* New York: Greenwillow.

———. 1995. *Lili on stage.* New York: Putnam.

Jonas, Ann. 1989. *Color dance.* New York: Greenwillow.

Kusugak, Michael Arvaarluk. 1993. *Northern lights: The soccer trails.* Art by Vladyana Krykorka. Toronto: Annick Press.

Lacapa, Kathleen, and Michael Lapaca. 1994. *Less than half, more than whole.* Illustrated by Michael Lacapa. 2d ed. Taylor, Ariz.: Storytellers Publishing House.

Lee, Jeanne M. 1991. *Silent lotus.* New York: Farrar.

Morris, Ann. 1996. *The daddy book.* Photographs by Ken Heyman. New York: Silver Press.

———. 1996. *The mommy book.* Photographs by Ken Heyman. New York: Silver Press.

Patrick, Denise Lewis. 1993. *Red dancing shoes.* Paintings by James E. Ransome. New York: Tambourine.

Smith, Cynthia Leitich. 2000. *Jingle dancer.* Illustrated by Cornelus Van Wright and Ying-Hwa Hu. New York: Morrow Junior Books.

Thomassie, Tynia. 1996. *Mimi's tutu*. Illustrated by Jan Spivey Gilchrist. New York: Scholastic.

Walrows, Merrill K., and Irisa Tekerean. 1989. *Art and writing throughout the year*. Torrence, Calif.: Frank Schaffer Publications.

Waters, Kate, and Madeline Slovenz-Low. 1990. *Lion dancer*. Photographs by Martha Cooper. New York: Scholastic.

Williams, Vera B. 1990. *More, more, more said the baby*. New York: Greenwillow.

Chapter 5

Community—We Are All Related

Guy's Perspective

In Native American cultures, community extends beyond neighborhood or geographical boundaries. Community includes people who share ideals, extend friendship, develop relationships, or influence one another's lives. Someone can live across town and be part of your community. Within the community, people care for one another. Among the Lakota people there is a teaching called the tiyospaye, *which means family and community. The tiyospaye is people taking care of one another.*

My father had a special room in the basement of our house that was well stocked with food. He would buy extra food from neighbors, such as vegetables from their gardens, even if our family didn't need the food. Periodically my dad would go down into the basement, fill a box with food, and tell us boys to take it over to Mrs. So-and-so. We would drive up to her house, leave the box of food on the porch, and drive away. For a long time I couldn't understand why my dad bought food and then just gave it away. Later, I understood. That was community. My father could care for his own family, but he also cared for his community.

Every year we take truckloads of clothing and school supplies from Ohio to the reservations in South Dakota. Last year, a little girl on one of the reservations gave me a picture she had painted with watercolors. "This is for you," she said. "Thank you." To me, all those people in Ohio who gave supplies, time, and financial support to the food and clothing drive are now part of her community. Community goes way beyond physical boundaries. What we do in Ohio affects people out West. People in South Dakota now know about Dayton and Cincinnati and have good feelings about the people in those places.

American Indian children are not always accepted into non-Native society. My youngest son's mother is African American, and we live in a predominantly black community. I've noticed that my son is not invited to play basketball and football by the neighborhood children because he is viewed as Indian, and in their minds, Indians don't play sports. When he goes to the reservation, though, all the children want him to play because they see him as black, and African American people are regarded as great athletes. Among his relatives, though, he's accepted as being Indian.

💲 💲 💲

Sally's Perspective

One day during lunch a child at my table asked me what I planned to do over the weekend. This was a reversal of the typical conversation, since I am the one who usually asks the children what they plan to do. In this case, I had an exciting event I anticipated attending, and I shared this with the children. I told them that I was going to a Native American art show, and I was really excited about it. Much to my surprise, the faces of all five of the children at the table immediately fell.

"Don't go," one child told me. "Indians are bad."

"Yeah," said another child. "They'll kill you."

"Please don't go," said a third. "We'll never see you again."

Naturally, I was troubled by their reaction. I told them that I most definitely planned to go and meet these talented artists. Not only would I be back on Monday, but I would bring the class a present from the art show.

On Monday I brought to school an autographed print of Cherokee artist James Oberle's painting "The Heartbeat of Turtle Island" (the painting that appears on the cover of this book). I asked the children to look at the picture and tell me what they saw. Right away the children noticed four people and four colors, red, white, black, and yellow, arranged around a circle. They quickly observed that the people were on *the back of a turtle, which stretched into the dark sky. "The turtle must be protecting the people," one child said. Then another child remarked that there was a small turtle inside the circle of people. "The people must be protecting that turtle," she said. The children had noticed an important aspect of the painting that I had initially missed, the small turtle at the center of the circle. We read the inscription written to the children from the artist: "To the children of Arlitt/Best wishes/James Oberle." They no longer seemed afraid of Indians.*

Building on Similarities

All of us are part of communities, whether urban, suburban, or rural. In addition, we are usually members of many smaller groups, such as neighborhoods, schools, religious organizations, clubs, and sporting teams. As part of communities, we share benefits and responsibilities with the other members. For example, if we become sick or hurt, we have doctors in our community to help us, as well as ambulances in emergencies and friends and neighbors who might bring us food. On the other hand, we can help our communities stay healthy by not throwing trash on the ground and by interacting safely with one another. These are aspects of community that children can begin to understand because of their daily experiences. Teachers can help children realize that although communities may look different, they share the common quality of people helping and enjoying one another.

Appreciating Differences

Many of us live in communities that partition themselves in some areas as much as they intersect in others. If we look more closely, we may find specific "community" events that are attended by different groups. For example, in Cincinnati, some musical and cultural events are attended almost entirely by African American citizens, while other events attract primarily white attendees. Why does this happen? Children may also notice that they live in neighborhoods of predominantly one race or culture. What does this signify? In school, we can help children build a comfort level and interest in diverse cultures by introducing music, art, stories, and images of many peoples.

We can assist children in understanding the unique aspects of cultures while still emphasizing their overall similarities. In this way, we prepare children to share the larger communities of city, state, country, and world.

Incorporating Native American Perspectives into Curriculum

Communities and Animals

Andy, an Alaskan Tale, by Susan Welsh-Smith, illustrated by Rie Muñoz

Most children have had experiences with animals in their communities. Even if they don't have pets of their own, they notice birds, squirrels, rabbits, and other local animals. *Andy, an Alaskan Tale* was written by Susan Welsh-Smith, who is the education coordinator for the Ninilchik Traditional Council in Alaska. The book introduces children to an Inuit community through the antics of a large English sheepdog, Andy. He arrives in a small airplane along with his owners, the new schoolteachers. The children quickly come to love Andy, who looks very different from their sled dogs. With his furry gray hair, he reminds them of an elder. Then one day Andy is lost. Since he doesn't know how to find his way around the frozen tundra, the teachers are very worried, and everyone in the community begins to search for him. The word "Andy" fills the page as all of the children call his name. The story ends happily when Andy arrives home, riding on a snowmobile from a neighboring community.

Children often see unappealing, inaccurate images of "Eskimos," even in school materials and books. The curriculum typically focuses on perceived oddities, such as eating blubber and living in igloos. Many children respond by saying "gross," and decide "Eskimos" are uncivilized or stupid. *Andy, an Alaskan Tale* goes a long way toward countering those images. Children see

Native children much like themselves who care for a funny dog and help in his rescue. The Inuit children live in houses, go to school, build snowmen, throw snowballs, and have skis and sleds. These are all aspects of community that bridge differences by building on similarities.

Writing—Animal Stories

This is me — getting ice cream with a dog.

Children often ask to have *Andy, an Alaskan Tale* read many times to them. Teachers might follow up on interest in this book by having children write stories about animals they are familiar with. Children who have pets may wish to write about their experiences with them. Other children may choose to describe animals they notice living around them, such as pigeons, squirrels, or mice. Depending on their writing level, teachers may encourage children to write their own words or dictate their stories. The animal stories can be compiled into a class book to share with the group. This helps to build a sense of community within the classroom since everyone can participate in the group project.

Blocks—Arctic Animals

After reading *Andy, an Alaskan Tale*, children may be interested in learning about some of the animals that live in the Arctic. Plastic Arctic animals can be added to the block area, along with authentic pictures of animals and people from the area. Polar bears, seals, walruses, and whales are all available in early childhood catalogs or toy stores. Children can create their own stories with the animals or reenact favorite books. Teachers might place a copy of *Andy, an Alaskan Tale* in the block area to encourage children to re-create the story.

Math—Doggie Grid Game

Andy, an Alaskan Tale often spurs interest in dogs. Teachers can extend this interest to the math area by designing a related grid game. Math grid games consist of bingo-type cards used in combination with dice and interesting counters. In this game, the grid boards consist of four rows of snowflake stickers, five stickers per row, mounted on dark-blue poster board, 10 by 8 inches.

The counters are small plastic dogs, available in toy stores, party supply stores, or teacher catalogues. Children play the game by rolling a die, quantifying the dots, and collecting a corresponding number of dogs for their board. Teachers of younger preschool children can simplify the game by reducing the number of dots on the die. Using a 1-inch cube for the die, teachers can adhere from one to three small, round stickers on each side of the cube. Smaller amounts are easier for younger or less experienced children to quantify. Teachers of older children can use two dice and let the children add them together. Teachers might decide to include additional counters, such as small cardboard bones.

Children could collect one dog and one bone for each sticker. The game boards should be laminated for durability.

Communities and Counting

My Arctic 1,2,3, by Michael Arvaarluk Kusugak, illustrated by Vladyana Kryskorka

Children are usually familiar with the counting book genre of literature. This book gives them the opportunity to count animal inhabitants of another part of the world, the Arctic. Inuit author Michael Arvaarluk Kusugak explains that in his community there are no trees, no highways, no fences, no farms, and no zoos, but there are lots of animals. Clear illustrations include a polar bear, ringed seals, killer whales, bowhead whales, arctic foxes, and *siksiks,* or small ground squirrels. Illustrated material at the end of the book provides descriptions of the animals and explains their relationship to the Native people.

Social Studies and Math—Neighborhood Walk

Sometimes we don't devote enough attention to inhabitants of our own communities. After reading *My Arctic 1,2,3,* teachers may decide to take children on a walk through their school community. What animals live around the school? How many of each can they find? What kinds of trees and plants are part of the community? What types of houses, buildings, or stores can they find? Who lives and works in their community? Children can keep notebooks of the people, animals, plants, and buildings they find in their community. Teachers can record the observations of children who are not yet old enough to write them. After returning to school, children may wish to share their notes and make their own community counting books.

Literature—Alphabet Books

Alphabet books are similar in style to counting books. Instead of associating quantities of objects with numerals, children form relationships between letters and objects that start with them. Several alphabet books deal with materials specific to Native cultures or indigenous to their part of the country.

Navajo ABC: A Diné Alphabet Book, by Luci Tapahonso (Diné) and Eleanor Schick, shows materials from the Diné culture of the Southwest. The authors explain in the foreword that all of the objects and words in this alphabet book are only parts of larger ideas, which are expressed through stories, songs, and prayers. Included in the colorful illustrations are words such as *arroyo, cradleboard, fry bread, hooghan, loom, turquoise, sheep, uncle, velvet,* and *yucca.* The glossary includes definitions of all the words, as well as a pronunciation guide.

A Is for Aloha, by Stephanie Feeney, with photos by Hella Hammid, uses the ABC format to portray some of the people, places, and experiences that are part of the lives of Hawaiian children. The illustrations, which are large black and white photographs, include many

Native Hawaiian children and families. Examples of words used in the book are *aloha, beach, canoe, gecko, hibiscus, lei, tutu,* and *ukulele.* A section at the end of the book includes definitions and pronunciations.

K Is for Kiss Good Night, by Jill Sardegna, with pictures by Michael Hays, is a multicultural alphabet book. Beautiful illustrations show children of several races being put to bed by loving parents. The book clearly accentuates an important similarity among all peoples—the love parents have for their children. The alphabet letters are associated with the first letter of a short phrase, such as "dreams forming in my head" for the letter D and "night-light glowing softly" for N. This is a very soothing book to use before naptime.

Writing Center—Community Animals

After reading *My Arctic 1,2,3* and exploring animals in their own community, children may wish to write their own community animal books. The class writing center is the perfect place to organize supportive materials.

Word Cards—Teachers should start by talking with the class about what animals they have seen in the community. This will help determine which word cards to include in the area. Carefully print the animal words on 3 by 5-inch index cards and illustrate them with a drawing, sticker, or computer clip art. Since some children may also wish to write about animals from *My Arctic 1, 2, 3,* word cards of those animals can also be included.

Fancy Pencils—Animal pencil toppers may entice some children to write. Pencil toppers can be found in school supply stores and catalogues as well as in party supply stores. Be sure to select lightweight pencil toppers. The heavier rubber type make it difficult for young children to support the pencils.

Sentence Fill-in Strips—The sentence below, preprinted on strips of paper, may encourage children to copy word cards and write numerals.

I saw _____ _____ *outside.*

Children can fill in the first blank with a numeral and the second blank with the name of an animal. Teachers can print the sentence by hand or type it on a computer, using a large point size and a font that looks like standard print. Teachers may wish to display a sample sentence strip already filled out as a guideline.

Blank Books—Blank books to go with the writing center can be easily made ahead of time. Cut sheets of construction paper into thirds to create strips 4 inches high and 9 inches wide. These strips can be folded in half to form the front and back covers of each book. Cut inexpensive paper into similar strips and fold to form the inside pages. Staple the paper together to create the blank books. A sticker or rubber stamp impression of an animal can be used to decorate the covers.

Communities and Art Traditions

Earth Daughter, by George Ancona

George Ancona employs vivid photography to introduce readers to the community of Ácoma Pueblo, in what is now New Mexico. We learn about the culture, traditions, family life, and community events of this Pueblo culture through the activities of a young girl, Alicia. Children can compare her modern home in a nearby community with the ancient Pueblo home her family also maintains in Ácoma. Alicia runs cross-country races with her friends at school, collects stamps, shares meals with her family,

makes tortillas, and dances with her mother and clan in traditional cere-monies. Much of *Earth Daughter* focuses on the traditional art of pottery, for which Ácoma Pueblo is known worldwide. Alicia learns the art from her grandmother, and we are able to follow every step of the process, from the collection of the clay to the final firing of the product, through spectacular photographic illustrations. Alicia and her family maintain their cultural tra-ditions in a modern world. "When I grow up," Alicia tells us, "I want to be a potter and also go to college to become a lawyer."

Earth Daughter gives children vivid images of a community that may be very different from their own. On the other hand, there are also many similarities. Children relate positively to Alicia because she is a modern child cared for by a loving family. She engages in hobbies that are similar to those of many children in our classrooms. Because many bonds of commonality are firmly established in the book, children accept and appreciate Alicia's special talents and cultural heritage in a way that often does not happen when only differ-ences are highlighted.

Art—Clay Creations

Clay work is becoming increasingly popular in school classrooms, in part due to the influence of the Reggio Emilia schools in Italy. As teachers observe the touring displays of the young Italian children's art and clay creations, they become interested in providing similar experiences for their classes. *Earth Daughter* is a natural tie-in for children working with clay. They can compare techniques and designs of the Ácoma pottery with those of potters in their own community, as well as with their own creations. Teachers should encourage children to create their own designs and images. Symbols and designs used on Ácoma pottery are unique to that culture and have special meaning for the Pueblo people who produce it.

Field Trip—Visiting a Local Potter

After reading *Earth Daughter* and beginning to work with clay themselves, children may be excited to visit a local potter. The artist can show the children different types of clay, demonstrate a variety of techniques, and perhaps assist the children with their own creations. Another resource for observing more advanced clay work might be a local high school or university art program. Older students may be excited to demonstrate their skills and help younger children work with clay.

Communities and Ceremonies

Cheryl's Potlatch, by Sheila Thompson

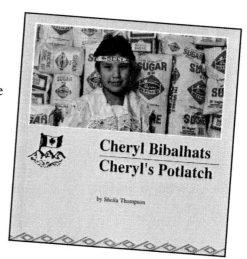

Cheryl's Potlatch describes a naming ceremony and potlatch given in honor of a young girl of the Caribou Clan, Lake Babine Band, Carrier Nation. Potlatches are celebrations held at important times that bring all of the community together. The story is told through Cheryl's own words and illustrated with colorful photographs, interspersed with line drawings. Cheryl explains that it is a special day for her because she gets a new name. Her friends at school will still know her as Cheryl, but she will now also have an Indian name. Cheryl also describes her Native community, which is composed of clans. She explains the giving tradition of the potlatch and shares her excitement that now it is her family's turn to do the giving.

Teachers may be interested to note that potlatches were banned by the Canadian government in 1887. Both the United States and Canadian governments outlawed all ceremonies because they wanted Indian peoples to assimilate. Subsequently, potlatch celebrations went "underground" and were observed in remote locations. Laws banning potlatches were repealed in 1951.

Writing—Special Days

Many cultures celebrate special days honoring an individual's growth in relationship to community values. Examples include religious ceremonies, such as baptisms and bar mitzvahs, school graduations, and weddings. Ask children to think about ceremonies they may have attended. Were gifts exchanged, as at Cheryl's potlatch? If so, who did the giving and who received the gifts? Children can write about celebrations they are familiar with and share their stories with the class.

Communities and the Arts

A Rainbow at Night: The World in Words and Pictures by Navajo Children, by Bruce Hucko

Bruce Hucko is an art educator who spent ten years working with children on the Navajo Reservation as an Artist-in-Education with the Utah Arts Council and the National Endowment for the Arts. In *A Rainbow at Night,* he has compiled the paintings, drawings, and reflections of twenty-three Navajo (Diné) children, ages five to eleven. Each work of art is reproduced in vivid color and accompanied by a photograph of the child who created it, the child's descriptions or reflections about the artwork, and related information about Navajo culture. In addition, art instructor Bruce Hucko suggests art projects that invite children to reflect on their own cultures and traditions as they create. For example, one young artist in the book draws inspiration from her exposure to Navajo rug weaving and draws a geometric, brilliantly colored "Rainbow Rug." As a related activity, Hucko suggests that children look around them for objects with strong pattern or design and use them as a basis for their own creations. Another child featured in *A Rainbow at Night* incorporates a grinding stone, vase, sagebrush, and flowers into her painting. The author encourages children to choose objects that are special for them, arrange the objects in an interesting way, and then draw or paint them.

A Rainbow at Night connects children of all cultures through art. The children's reflections, combined with descriptions of their culture and community, help all of us gain deeper insights into the culture and beliefs of the Diné people. Since most children naturally like to draw and describe their pictures, they are interested in seeing what these Diné children have created, as well as hearing their reflections about their drawings and paintings. The photographic portraits of the young artists provide real-life images for children in our classrooms to identify with. The children in *A Rainbow at Night* are not stereotypes. They are real children, much like those in our classrooms.

Literature and Art—Class Stories

Teachers will find numerous ideas from author and artist Bruce Hucko to guide children in their own creations. Teachers may wish to focus on a particular work of art in the book that seems especially appealing to a group of children. The children can talk about the drawing or painting, and the teacher can implement the suggestions provided by Hucko. For example, accompanying a pencil and watercolor drawing titled "Navajo Scarecrow," Hucko writes, "What marks the boundary of your backyard? Look on your own land and find an important object that marks a side or corner of your property. It could be a tree, a rock, a garden, a wall or fence. Draw it. Add lines to show texture and what is in the background." After completing their artwork, children can write or dictate their reflections, much like the children in *A Rainbow at Night*.

Art—Native American Artists

It is especially valuable for children to view and discuss the artwork of authentic Native artists, as well as artists from other cultures. Artists' reproductions are often available at affordable prices. Festivals, Native American stores, galleries, libraries, and Web sites are places to look for Native artwork. Check chapter 8 for a listing of American Indian artists. Teachers should remember that many of the children's books suggested throughout this book are illustrated by Native artists. These illustrations may provide a good starting point for talking about Native art. In addition, many artists are featured on Web sites. Using an Internet search engine, teachers can enter the artist's name and view examples of artwork and prices.

Not Recommended

1. Copying Native American art

Sometimes teachers fall into the trap of encouraging children to copy another culture's art forms. While it is important for children to view art from many different cultures, children's own artwork should come from their own traditions. Often there is symbolism and spirituality underlying a culture's art traditions that people who are not a part of that culture may not be aware of. For this reason, teachers should not encourage children to create Native American art, such as Navajo weavings or sand paintings. Rather, they can help children appreciate the artwork by showing them photos or actual pieces of art and then guiding them in their own art explorations.

2. Adopting symbols from another culture

"Indian symbols" are commercially very popular. We see representations on everything from flowerpots to T-shirts to kitchen curtains. Teachers often purchase activity books that reproduce these so-called symbols and suggest that children use them in their artwork. This is supposed to help children understand Native American (note the singular) culture. There are many problems with this approach. For one, symbols are specific to particular Native cultures. Since there are no global Native American symbols, portraying "Indian" symbols as universal misinforms children. It perpetuates the myth that there is one Native American culture rather than hundreds. Another problem relates to adopting another culture's symbols. Native symbols are often viewed as sacred. While a person knowledgeable in the culture can use them in a respectful and appropriate way, others may unknowingly degrade the culture through misrepresentations or applications. We want to encourage children to respect other cultures, not offend them.

One final note needs to be mentioned in terms of legality. The Indian Arts and Crafts Act of 1990, Public Law 101-644, prevents the marketing of products identified as "Indian made" when they are not actually made by Indian people.

3. Counting or alphabet books with stereotypical images

Teachers should be especially alert to stereotypical images in counting and alphabet books. For example, in one well-known counting book, *I Can Count*, by Dick Bruna, children count the feathers on an "Indian" child's headband. This is the type of stereotypical image we need to leave out of the classroom.

References

Ancona, George. 1995. *Earth daughter*. New York: Simon & Schuster.

Bruna, Dick. 1975. *I can count*. New York: Methuen Children's Books Limited.

Feeney, Stephanie. 1980. *A is for aloha*. Photos by Hella Hammid. Honolulu: University of Hawaii Press.

Hucko, Bruce. 1996. *A rainbow at night: The world in words and pictures by Navajo children*. San Francisco: Chronicle Books.

Kusugak, Michael Arvaarluk. 1999. *My arctic 1,2,3*. Art by Vladyana Krykorka. Toronto: Annick Press.

Sardegna, Jill. 1994. *K is for kiss good night*. Pictures by Michael Hays. New York: Doubleday.

Tapahonso, Luci, and Eleanor Schick. 1995. *Navajo ABC: A Diné alphabet book*. Illustrations by Eleanor Schick. New York: Simon & Schuster.

Thompson, Sheila. 1994. *Cheryl's potlatch*. Vanderhoof, B.C., Canada: Yinka Dene Language Institute.

Welsh-Smith, Susan. 1991. *Andy, an Alaskan tale*. Illustrated by Rie Muñoz. New York: Cambridge University Press.

Zielbauer, Paul. 1999. Judge rules school district erred on religion in classrooms. *The New York Times*, 22 May, B1.

Chapter 6

The Environment—Celebrating the Circle of Life

Guy's Perspective

For Indian people, important teachings come from the earth. The earth is our Bible, our science book, and our health book, and the animals, plants, fish, and birds all have something to teach. I was introduced to books and written words when I went to school, and for a while, I lost my perspective on oral teaching. I thought that learning and teaching only came from the words in books. I remember asking one of my uncles where our Lakota teachings came from. I wondered if we had any commandments like the ones we had read at school. My uncle replied, "Indian people believe God made one mistake. He gave people the ability to think. Everything else has a reason and a purpose." Then he showed me the differences in the bark and leaves of various trees and explained their purpose.

As time went on, I began to look for life's lessons in creation and to see a balance in nature. Everything in nature has a purpose. People may ask, "How can poison ivy be beneficial? What purpose does it have?" When you really observe poison ivy, you find that it keeps certain insects away from the plants that grow near it, like broadleaf, and those plants are beneficial. Poison ivy is their protector. So I began to see a balance in all things and the importance of maintaining it.

Through observing nature, Indian people developed an understanding of the circle of life that is still taught to their children. For example, the Lakota people noticed that after a prairie fire, the new plants came back fuller than ever, and this attracted the buffalo. From these observations, they learned to set fires to draw the buffalo to where they wanted them.

Today, Indian parents and uncles still teach their children what to watch for as they explore the outdoors. I can remember my mom saying, "You boys leave those plums alone. They're not ready yet." She would remind us, "The wild turnips already have their flowers, so you boys better not eat them." We were taught that once the turnips had their flowers, they were ready to seed. If you eat them then, there are no turnips for the next year. Plums, potatoes, turnips, sand berries, choke cherries, buffalo cherries, grapes, and mushrooms all grew wild. We knew where to get them and when they went into season.

Of course, sometimes we learned on our own. One time my brother and I were really anxious for rhubarb, but it was still green. We ate some anyway and got sick. Then Mom wanted to know what was wrong with us. "You boys know better than to eat green rhubarb," she told us. Sometimes we just had to learn the hard way. We were allowed to explore, though, and we learned to use nature to our best advantage while still maintaining balance.

$ $ $

Sally's Perspective

It was autumn, and in class we were talking about harvest and changes in the environment. I had placed dried corn in the science area along with a mortar and pestle. I wanted the children to experiment with grinding the corn and changing it into powder. Madison entered the area and began to pound corn with the pestle. After a short time, I approached and sat down next to her. I planned to say some of my teacher things, like "What is happening to the corn?" Before I could open my mouth, Madison turned and said, "You can't come in here. You're not Indian. Only Indians can grind corn." I was momentarily speechless. Here I was, closed out of one of the areas in my own classroom because of my race, by a child who was whiter than I was. I soon realized what was going on. Madison had recently seen the movie Pocahontas. *Based on the limited perspective of Indian people provided by the movie, she had decided that only Indians grind corn. Since she herself was grinding corn, she felt free to designate herself as Indian, but I was white and not grinding corn, so I didn't qualify. I told Madison that anyone could grind corn and I would like a turn too.*

Building on Similarities

All of us share the planet earth and are affected by our environment every day of our lives. We experience weather and seasonal changes, watch the growing and dying of plants, and notice the coming and going of various types of animals. Some of us may compare days when it is easy to breathe with those that smell "stinky." Children are also attuned to their environment. Most love playing outside. They watch bugs walking and flying, dig into the ground to find worms, pick dandelions and clover, trace the cracks in the ground with sticks, add water to dust to make mud, and watch the clouds. Children are fascinated by migrating flocks of birds, thunderstorms, and the first snowfall. They ask many questions. Because of this innate interest of children in nature, most teachers coordinate some of their curriculum around seasons of the year. Many also talk to children about caring for the environment and recycling. We are becoming increasingly aware of how the environment links the entire planet. In 2001 (Schmid), newspapers reported that drought in Northern Africa had produced huge dust clouds that traveled around the earth to deposit African soil in the United States. The environment is clearly something we all share.

Appreciating Differences

Although the environment affects all of us, there are notable cultural differences in the way people view the relationship between the land and its inhabitants. To Native peoples, there is a spiritual connection to Enemaka, or Mother Earth in the Lakota language, and a deep understanding of the importance of earth to our survival. For this reason, Indian people learned long ago not to pollute the water they drank from. Many people today, though, have the attitude that they can dump things into a river to be washed away. Not much thought is given to the people and animals living downstream. This contrasts sharply with a traditional Native view of the earth as sacred. In addition, among Native cultures, the earth is regarded as belonging to all, like the air we breathe, and not something to be owned. This is a very different perspective from the European idea of individual land ownership.

Incorporating Native American Perspectives into Curriculum

The Environment and the Cycle of Life

Did You Hear Wind Sing Your Name? by Sandra De Coteau Orie, with illustrations by Christopher Canyon

Did You Hear Wind Sing Your Name? is a celebration of the circle of life and spring rebirth. Oneida author Sandra De Coteau Orie describes the book as a song of thanks and invites the reader to sing along. The text is indeed lyrical and reflects the Oneida worldview. For example, one page reads, "Did you trace Turtle's tracks along the Creek and know you weren't alone?" The brilliantly colored double-page illustrations are breathtaking. They entice children to look at the book over and over again. While *Did You Hear Wind Sing Your Name?* describes objects that are familiar to children, such as flowers, new leaves on trees, and sunsets, it does so in a language that subtly conveys the Oneida worldview. The author provides background information about the Haudenosaunee (Iroquois) people and explains the significance of the plants and animals included in the book.

Science—Three Sisters Garden

In *Did You Hear Wind Sing Your Name?,* the author writes, "Did you see the fields of the Three Sisters coming?" She explains in the foreword that the Three Sisters are Corn, Beans, and Squash. They are considered vital to the Oneida people for sustaining their lives. Traditionally, they are planted together. The beans wrap around the corn stalks as they climb, and the spreading squash plants shield and protect the roots of the other plants. Children can plant a garden of beans, corn, and squash either outside or next to a window with lots of sunlight. They can compare the three types of seeds and how each plant looks as it grows. Children may wish to predict which seeds will sprout first, which will grow the tallest, and which will have the biggest leaves. Bean seeds planted in the spring often have beans before the end of the school year.

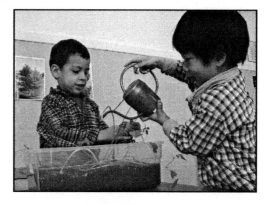

Music—Native American Flute

For thousands of years Native peoples have played flutes made from hollow plants or carved from red cedar. Lakota musician Tokeya Inajin (Kevin Locke) describes flute music as a way to capture the essence of the wind. He explains that cedar has great spiritual importance among Native peoples. When making a flute, the craftsman must remove the heart of the wood. The musician must then put his or her own heart back into the flute.

Native American flute music is hauntingly beautiful and very soothing. A notable recording is Kevin Locke's *Dream Catcher.* Accompanying the lovely flute music are sounds of nature, such as waves, thunder, birds, crickets, and frogs. Pieces include "Whispers on the Wind," "Circle of Life," and "The Earth Is My Blanket." Sally often played this recording in the art area of her classroom. Children enjoyed listening to the lyrical music as they drew or painted.

Art—Watercolor Paintings

Did You Hear Wind Sing Your Name? is a feast for the eyes. Nature is vividly depicted through the brilliantly painted illustrations. Children also like to paint what they see in nature. Teachers can help them reflect on their observations by bringing nature items into the classroom and displaying them on

an art table. Examples might include pussy willows, spring flowers, or a tree branch with blossoms or new leaves. Children can use watercolor paints to represent the plants. A copy of *Did You Hear Wind Sing Your Name?* might also be placed in the area to encourage children to look at the illustrations. Teachers can mount and display the children's paintings near the flower and plant arrangements they used as models.

Social Studies and Science—Spring in Our Community

Many teachers take nature walks in the fall to collect leaves or help children notice the change in seasons. While the weather in spring is less predictable in some parts of the country than in autumn, spring can actually be a wonderful time for a nature field trip. Children can see plants poking through the ground, just beginning to grow. They may also notice returning flocks of birds, caterpillars, nest building, wild flowers, and the first insects beginning to emerge. Teachers may decide to take along umbrellas in case of a sprinkle.

Keep the environment clean. Collect the trash.

Math—Recycling Game

This game integrates environmental issues with math concepts. The game board consists of a picture of a beautiful nature scene, perhaps from a calendar, mounted on poster board and laminated. The game pieces are tiny novelty food containers, found in party supply stores. Each player has a small plastic garbage can. The game begins with all of the food containers dumped on the nature scene. The object of the game is to pick up the trash. Players take turns rolling a die to determine how many pieces of trash they can put into their garbage can. The game ends when all the trash has been cleaned up. Players can quantify how many pieces of trash they have collected and sort it into categories, such as soda bottles, cereal boxes, and ice-cream cups.

The Environment and Trees

$ $ $

Guy's Perspective

The trees tell us in advance about the weather. On hot days, the leaves at the ends of the branches curl up to protect themselves, while on rainy days, they turn upward to catch the moisture. My dad taught us to read the leaves. I remember him saying one day, "Boys, don't be hanging out at the river all day. It's going to rain." We wondered what he was talking about. There was bright sunshine and no clouds. Of course, it did rain, and we got caught. There was a bad thunderstorm, and we got pelted with hail. My dad was livid. We asked him how he had known it would rain, and then he told us the signs to look for.

$ $ $

The Big Tree and the Little Tree, as told by Mary Augusta Tappage, edited by Jean E. Speare, illustrated by Terry Gallagher

Most children, even those in urban environments, have some familiarity with trees. Trees are fascinating. In many parts of the country, they change dramatically with every season of the year. In *The Big Tree and the Little Tree,* Mary Augusta Tappage tells a story from her Shuswap and Metis heritage of two evergreen trees growing in a forest. The big tree is proud and boastful and doesn't like having the little tree grow near him. He brags about feeding the squirrels, housing the birds' nests, and providing branches for the people, while the little tree is useless. But over time, the little tree grows big and strong, and the big tree becomes old and begins to die. The big tree now feels sad and useless. Instead of gloating, the young tree helps him reflect on his life and celebrate his achievements.

The Big Tree and the Little Tree sends a powerful message about the interdependence of us all. The detailed black and white line drawings richly support the text. Even young children understand the meaning of love, tolerance, and caring portrayed in this book.

Emma and the Trees, by Lenore Keeshig-Tobias, with illustrations by Polly Keeshig-Tobias, Ojibway translation by Rose Nadjiwon

Emma and the Trees, written by Ojibway storyteller Lenore Keeshig-Tobias, begins with a young girl, Emma, having a bit of a tantrum. In desperation, her mother points at the trees and tells Emma they are waving at her. Emma stops crying and begins to observe the trees. She notices that wherever she goes, the trees still wave at her. Soon she is waving back. Since *Emma and the Trees* is written in both English and Ojibway, children have the opportunity to see what the story looks like in another language.

Story Reenactment— Tree Puppets

The Big Tree and the Little Tree is a great story to tell, perhaps with puppets to act it out. Teachers can easily make evergreen tree puppets of various sizes out of green felt. They can be mounted to flat sticks, such as rulers or yardsticks, to

make them easier to hold up. At the beginning of the story, a large and a small tree are needed. As the story progresses, teachers may wish to use intermediate sizes of trees to represent the growing evergreen. Additional props, such as squirrels and birds, can also be cut from felt and added to the tree. Children love to help tell the story as they watch the puppets.

Science—Tree Observations

Both *The Big Tree and the Little Tree* and *Emma and the Trees* encourage children to make closer observations of trees, which can be incorporated into science activities or discussions centered around a tree project. With teacher direction, children

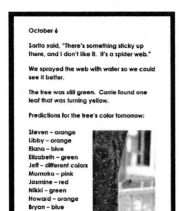

October 6

Sarita said, "There's something sticky up there, and I don't like it. It's a spider web."

We sprayed the web with water so we could see it better.

The tree was still green. Carrie found one leaf that was turning yellow.

Predictions for the tree's color tomorrow:

Steven – orange
Libby – orange
Elana – blue
Elizabeth – green
Jeff – different colors
Momoko – pink
Jasmine – red
Nikki – green
Howard – orange
Bryan – blue
Lucas – green

may begin to notice new insects and animals coming to live in a particular tree, as well as changes in the tree itself. Teachers might decide to start a tree observation project at the beginning of a new season, such as spring or fall. Children can describe a tree on their playground or close to their school, and the teacher can record their observations. Photographs can also be taken of the tree. The teacher can then ask children to predict what the tree will look like the following day. Some children, anticipating a change, come up with some remarkable ideas that show their limited remembrances of previous years. For example, in one class, children repeatedly predicted that the leaves on a tree on their playground would turn blue or pink by the following day. Each day children can write or dictate their observations and make predictions for the following day. When a dramatic change begins to occur, such as blossoms or leaves forming on the tree, children are more acutely aware of the transformation because their attention has remained focused on the tree over time.

Science—Tree Display

While most children have the opportunity to look at trees, many have never compared the feel of trees or looked at the inside of a tree. A tree display in the science area gives children the opportunity to discover more information about trees. Teachers might start by displaying pictures of trees along with samples of various types of bark for children to compare. For example, the paper bark of a white birch is very different from the thick, rougher bark of an oak tree. Next, teachers might add a cross-section of a tree trunk so children can examine the rings. (Craft stores often sell tree segments for making plaques.) Teachers can also bring in branches so that children can explore how they fork into smaller and smaller limbs and twigs. If possible, a small potted tree could be added to the area so children can observe the roots, trunk, branches, and leaves. Such firsthand explorations of trees make a far greater impact on children than just looking at pictures or reading about them in books.

Writing Center—Trees

Children may wish to continue their interest in trees by writing about them. A writing center related to trees encourages children to copy words and write stories.

Word Cards—Teachers should take their cues from the children as to what words to include on word cards. Some classes may be especially interested in the names of trees, such as maple, pine, or oak, while others may have more interest in color words to correspond to the changing color of the leaves. Generic words such as tree and leaf will probably be needed. Carefully print the words on 3 by 5-inch index cards and illustrate them with a drawing, sticker, or computer clip art to help children independently read them. Laminate the word cards for durability. They can be displayed in a basket or held upright in nametag holders.

Blank Books—Children like to write in blank books that have interesting shapes. Stencils or die cuts of leaf shapes, which teachers can use as a pattern for the books, can be found in craft stores. Cut the front and back covers out of an appropriate color of construction paper and the inside pages out of inexpensive or free paper. Staple the books together to create writing journals for children.

Jeff saw Maple trees waving.

Sentence Fill-Ins—Throughout the book *Emma and the Trees,* trees seem to be waving at the little girl. The action of the trees can be the basis of a predictable fill-in strip, such as the one below, to facilitate children's writing endeavors. Teachers can preprint the strips by hand or on a computer. Children can write their name in the first space and the name or color of a tree in the second space of the fill-in strip.

_____ *saw* _____ *trees waving.*

Art—Leaf Tiles

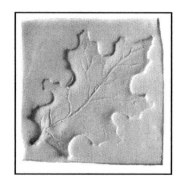

Creating leaf impressions in clay helps children observe the shapes of various leaves as well as their vein structure. Children start by rolling pieces of self-hardening clay into slabs about ¼-inch thick with wooden rollers or dowels. Each child places a leaf on the clay and rolls over it with a roller. Finally, the children carefully peel the leaves from the clay to reveal the impressions left behind. After the clay has dried, children can paint their leaves with watercolor or acrylic paint.

The Environment and Winter

SkySisters, by Jan Bourdeau Waboose, illustrated by Brian Deines

In *SkySisters,* two Anishinawbe (Ojibway) sisters share the excitement of a nighttime journey as they follow a tradition handed down through generations. Together, with the older sister leading the younger, they revel in the stillness of the night, the animals they glimpse, their frolics in the snow, the sounds of a coyote's song, and finally the beauty of the SkySpirits, or northern lights. Nishinaube Ojibway author Jan Bourdeau Waboose explores the bonds between sisters, their love of the northern landscape, and the close connection between humans and nature that is celebrated in their culture. The illustrator uses radiant oil paintings to represent the rich colors of the northern night.

Children respond to many aspects of this book. Many have siblings and can identify with the bonds between the sisters. Perhaps an older brother or sister also looks out for them and sometimes takes them on adventures. Children also love the games the girls play in the nighttime snow. They eagerly relate their own experiences with sucking icicles, catching snowflakes, holding hands and spinning around, and making snow angels on the ground. As children explore the similarities between themselves and the characters in the story, they also notice the beautiful illustrations of two Native American girls and their mother. Non-Native children may notice that the expressive language is somewhat different from what they are accustomed to hearing, as in the passage, "...look up to see Grandmother Moon glimmering behind a thin cloud." This is very different from the stereotypical and inaccurate broken English they are so often exposed to in cartoons, movies, and many children's books about Native peoples. The Anishinawbe worldview expressed in this book is imbedded in relationships and experiences that transcend culture.

Writing—Nighttime Explorations

The girls in *SkySisters* get to take a special walk together under the nighttime sky. While children do most of their exploring in the daytime, all have had some experiences with their families that happened in the night. Ask the children to think about a special evening when they were out after dark. It might have been during a camping trip, on a car ride to look at holiday lights, or in

One time my family went to the zoo at night. It was the Festival of Lights. I saw a red fish in the dark water. He wasn't moving. I think he was asleep.

their own yard in the summer, listening to crickets and looking at fireflies. Children can write about their nighttime experiences and illustrate their stories.

Art—Crayon and Watercolor Drawings

Deep shades of purple and black overlay the illustrations in *SkySisters*. After reading the book, children may wish to make their own nighttime pictures. They can start by drawing images and scenery with crayons. Then they can paint over the entire picture with purple, dark blue, or black watercolor paints. Since the crayon resists the paint, the drawings show through the paint overlay. Children may wish to look at some of the illustrations in *SkySisters* to see how artist Brian Deines blends colors. The children's pictures can be mounted and displayed, perhaps along with their stories about nighttime adventures.

The Environment and Animals

There are many trickster personalities in Native American stories. These include coyote and weasel, from the four-leggeds; raven, from the birds; Iktomi (Lakota), the spider, from insects; and even people tricksters, such as

Nanabosho (Ojibway). The trickster characters represent both good and bad, depending upon the situation. Coyote was probably chosen to use in stories because he is so curious. Coyote watches and observes and learns. From coyote, Indian people learned the importance of watching. *Iktomi* is the word in Lakota for both spider and alcohol. Through Iktomi, you see things differently. Again, this is neither good nor bad, but varies with circumstances.

Ma'ii and Cousin Horned Toad, by Shonto Begay

Diné (Navajo) author Shonto Begay writes that Coyote stories are teaching tools used to describe appropriate ways of behaving and also explain natural phenomena. They are often very entertaining. Coyote is called Ma'ii in the Diné language. The story of *Ma'ii and Cousin Horned Toad* was told to Begay by his grandmother when he was a child. It explores the relationship between greed and balance, effort and prosperity. In this tale Ma'ii, or Coyote, is hungry and tricks Toad out of the corn he has worked hard to grow and cook. Toad, of course, has the last laugh, and Coyote learns a lesson. Children are intrigued by the antics of Coyote and cheer for the resilient Toad. Primary-age children are also ready to discuss the underlying meaning of the story and relate the lessons to their own experiences.

Morning on the Lake, by Jan Bourdeau Waboose, illustrated by Karen Reczuch

Another book that explores animals in the natural environment is Jan Bourdeau Waboose's *Morning on the Lake.* This book is very different from the trickster tale by Begay. A young Anishinawbe (Ojibway) boy and his grandfather share a special day and night as they explore a lake and forest. The book is really three interlinked stories. At dawn, as they head out into the lake in a canoe made by Grandfather, they observe a family of loons. The boy is reminded of the stories of loons handed down by his Ojibway ancestors. In the second story, which is titled "Noon," Grandfather and Grandson climb a rock cliff and are rewarded by a visit from an eagle. In the closing story, "Night," they are visited by a pack of wolves. In each story, the boy is frightened by his close encounters with the animals, but learns from his grandfather, who knows the animals well. The close ties among the Anishinawbe people, their traditional homeland, and the animals they share it with are very evident in this book. The illustrations by Karen Reczuch are stunning and show beautiful, loving images of Grandfather and Grandson.

Reading—Trickster Tales

Since many Native cultures have traditions of trickster tales, teachers may wish to introduce stories from other Native American authors. Children can enjoy the books and compare the various representations of the trickster character to Coyote in Begay's book. The Nanabosho books by Joseph McLellan (Ojibway) are examples of trickster tales. One of these books is described in the bibliography in chapter 8.

Science—Animal Explorations

Morning on the Lake introduces children to animals that are native to woodland areas of the northern United States and Canada. After reading about the close encounters between the child in the story and the animals in his environment, children can begin to study animals that share their locality. Teachers might start with a visit to a local nature preserve or park, many of which employ naturalists to facilitate field trips. Children can watch for animals near their school during outside times and also consult books about animals from their area. They can record their observations in journals to share with the rest of the class.

Not Recommended

1. Asking children to make up Indian stories

After reading a story from another culture, teachers sometimes ask children to write in the style or tradition of that culture. As teachers, we need to understand that traditional stories have deep cultural underpinnings that cannot be adequately understood and expressed by individuals who are not part of the culture. When we attempt to copy another culture's literature or art, we often unintentionally mock the very people we are hoping to better understand.

Teachers can help children appreciate literature by encouraging them to reflect about their own cultural backgrounds. In the case of traditional stories, teachers may ask children what stories their relatives have told to them. In some cases, the stories may extend back to Europe, such as many of the fairy tales children hear, or to Africa or Asia. While children should read material from authors of many backgrounds, they should be asked to write based on their own experiences or imaginings.

2. Referring to American Indians as environmentalists

While the "environmentalist" label may seem a positive one, it is still a stereotype when applied to specific groups of people. While many Native American people do remain closely connected to the natural environment, others do not. Teachers should not lead children to expect all Native Americans to fit a particular model.

References

Begay, Shonto. 1992. *Ma'ii and Cousin Horned Toad.* New York: Scholastic.

Keeshig-Tobias, Lenore. 1996. *Emma and the trees.* Illustrations by Polly Keeshig-Tobias. Ojibway translation by Rose Nadjiwon. Toronto: Sister Vision, Black Women and Women of Colour Press.

Locke, Kevin (Tokeya Inajin), performer. 1992. *Dream catcher.* Redway, Calif.: Earthbeat! EB–2696.

Orie, Sandra De Coteau. 1995. *Did you hear wind sing your name?* Illustrations by Christopher Canyon. New York: Walker and Company.

Schmid, Randolph E. (Associated Press). 2001. African dust poses risk to health and ecosystem. *Cincinnati Enquirer,* 2 July, A4.

Tappage, Mary Augusta, and Jean E. Speare. 1986. *The big tree and the little tree.* Illustrated by Terry Gallagher. Winnipeg: Pemmican Publications.

Waboose, Jan Bourdeau. 1997. *Morning on the lake.* Illustrated by Karen Reczuch. Toronto: Kids Can Press.

———. 2000. *SkySisters.* Illustrated by Brian Deines. Toronto: Kids Can Press.

Chapter 7

Family Heritage Project

Guy's Perspective

I remember going to grade school in Wakpala, South Dakota, and every day after school my mom would tell me to go check on my grandma. I'd run over to her house to make sure there was water in the bucket and wood by the stove. She would always ask me, "How was school? What did you learn about today?"

One day I asked my grandma where all the Indian people are today. We had just begun to study geography and history at school, and we saw a map of the United States with different tribes of Indian people all over the country. My whole world at that time was Wakpala, so when I looked at that map, I said, "Wow. There are Indian people all over." So I asked Grandma, "Where are they all at?" She took some time and asked me to sit down with her. "There are Indian people all over the world," she told me. It made me feel good thinking that the whole world was inhabited by Indians.

I always remembered that story. There was a point in my life, during my radical phase, when I decided that she was right. There are Indian people all over the world because of what people have done to indigenous populations—cultural genocide and separation from the land. But Grandma also told me that Indian people were just people. Today, a lot of people say that the word Lakota means friend or ally. My grandmother told me that Lakota means people, and there are people all over the world. What separates us is the terminology we use to classify each other.

Sally's Perspective

Chi-Hoon arrived at Monica's preschool classroom and ran straight to the class diaries. They were kept on a bookshelf next to the writing center of the classroom. The children in the class each had a diary containing photographs of them and their families, messages from their families, and art and writing projects from school. Chi-Hoon quickly found her own diary and those of several other children. She eagerly watched the door of the classroom until some other families arrived. Then, taking one of the parents by the hand, she led him to the writing table and "read" four class diaries to him. Each time she selected the diary of another child, she pointed that child out to the adult. Chi-Hoon repeated her practice of reading class diaries to parents for many days. It became one of her favorite activities.

The Family Heritage Project

During the 2000–2001 school year, five early childhood classrooms in the Cincinnati area undertook a long-range project to explore cultural and personal diversity. The Family Heritage Project introduced children to Native American artists and writers, whose work served as an inspiration for a study of the families and cultures of the children in the programs. The project provides an example of the principles advocated in this book: incorporating Native literature and art as part of the overall curriculum.

Throughout this book, we often advise teachers to help children understand diversity by first reflecting on their own roots and exploring their own cultures. The Family Heritage Project evolved from family explorations in several early childhood classrooms. The teachers were all interested in emergent curriculum and in individual and group projects such as those undertaken by the Reggio Emilia schools in Italy. Since they knew that their children liked to talk about their families, the teachers felt the project would help them better understand the similarities among all of their families, as well as the differences.

Five classrooms participated in the project: two preschool classes from the Arlitt Child and Family Research and Education Center at the University of Cincinnati and three kindergarten classes from the Fairfield City Schools, a suburban school district near Cincinnati. The preschool classes were very diverse, including children and families of different socioeconomic class backgrounds and many different races and nationalities. The preschool class taught by Monica Battle included three Korean children; one child from China; five African American children, of whom two were Muslim; one child from Argentina; and six European American children. The preschool class taught by Lowellette Lauderdale included three African American children; two Chinese children; one child from Pakistan; one Filipino child; and four European American children. The two preschool classes shared a classroom, with one class coming in the morning and the other in the afternoon. The kindergarten classes consisted of primarily European American children but included several African American children and a child from Mexico. A morning and an afternoon class were taught by Amy Mackey, and another morning class was taught by Melissa Adamson.

The teachers decided to embark on the Family Heritage Project while participating in a Reggio Emilia study group supported by the Ohio Department of Education for teachers interested in implementing projects in early childhood classrooms. They were able to support one another throughout the project, compare notes, and get ideas from one another. All four teachers shared similar goals:

- Explore diversity with children
- Incorporate Native American curricular materials into their programs
- Strengthen cultural roots and family awareness
- Integrate literacy and language development throughout the project
- Facilitate communication among all of the children
- Employ a variety of art media to strengthen and support the project
- Involve families as an integral part of the project

Resources and Inspiration

In order to help children think more deeply about their own families and communities, the teachers used several children's books, three of which were written by Native American authors or teachers working in Native American communities. These books were prominently displayed in the classrooms. They were used as resources throughout the project and gave both children and teachers ideas for how to proceed with further explorations of family.

This Land Is My Land, by George Littlechild

This book is a compilation of paintings by Cree artist George Littlechild. Littlechild often builds his artwork around photographs of his family or ancestors, and he uses his artwork to paint a personal and cultural history. Children are attracted to the bright colors and interesting forms in Littlechild's paintings. Teachers in the Family Heritage Project incorporated his technique of embedding photographs within his artwork. They photocopied pictures of each child's family and encouraged the children to combine the photos with various art media.

We Are All Related: A Celebration of Our Cultural Heritage, by Students of G. T. Cunningham Elementary School

This stunning book was an inspiration for the teachers in the Family Heritage Project. It documents how the students at G. T. Cunningham Elementary School in Vancouver explored their cultural heritage through interviews with parents and elders from their community. The Canadian project emphasized Native cultures, including stories, artwork, and traditional teachings. The children got to meet George Littlechild and view his show at the Tribal Art Gallery in Vancouver. Subsequently, the Vancouver children used various art media to depict their families and wrote reflections about their artwork. Photographs of the children, along with color representations of their artwork and their written documentation, are included in this beautiful book. In a similar manner, children in the Family Heritage Project discussed some of Littlechild's artwork in *This Land Is My Land* before using art media to represent their families and important events they had shared together. They dictated or wrote their reflections about their creations.

A Rainbow at Night: The World in Words and Pictures by Navajo Children, by Bruce Hucko

This book is similar to *We Are All Related*. It is a compilation of the paintings, drawings, and reflections of children from the Navajo (Diné) Reservation, assembled by their art instructor. Once again the culture and family heritage of the children is depicted through both words and artwork. This book was also used as a model by the teachers in the Family Heritage Project.

I Love My Mommy Because ... and *I Love My Daddy Because ...,* both by Laurel Porter-Gaylord, with pictures by Ashley Wolff

These books were used as an introduction to the project in the preschool classrooms in order to help children reflect on the importance of their parents to them. Using animal parents as examples, the author describes various ways that parents care for their young. The books provoked remembrances about their own parents among the children and led to inspired conversations.

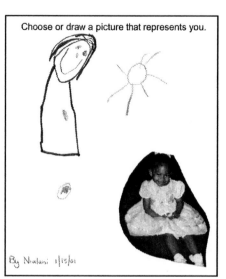

Choose or draw a picture that represents you.

By Nalani 1/15/01

Introducing the Project

Preschool

Before the project began, the teachers alerted parents by showing them the related children's books and describing their goals for the project. In Monica's class, this preparation took place during a parents' night. The

What did you do during winter break? Include a memento, drawing, or picture that represents your family traditions.

This is our Christmas tree with all the pretty and colorful ornaments. My mom is the one who decorated it. We also had lots of presents underneath. My whole family was at our house for Christmas.

parents were introduced to the Littlechild and Hucko books, and Monica talked about her goals for the project. The parents were already working on a family quilt for their class and were enthusiastic about this upcoming opportunity to participate further in a group endeavor. In Lowellette's class, parents received a letter describing the project and talked to her informally about it. Both classrooms had already initiated family diaries, in which the parents contributed photographs of their child, wrote a message to their child, and included a description of some of their child's summertime activities.

In both preschool classes, the project was introduced to the children during group time by the music teacher, who served as a consultant for the project. She began by singing a song that included each child's name and then read the book *I Love My Daddy Because ...* to the class. During the book sharing, the children compared characteristics of the animal daddies to their own daddies. For example, a page that features a lion father and cub reads, "He takes naps with me." Upon hearing this, Carlos commented that his father likes to take naps, too, but he snores loudly. The children were excited to talk about their daddies, and most eagerly chimed in.

Next, the teacher showed the children the painting "Give Thanks to the Grandmothers" from George Littlechild's book, *This Land Is My Land,* and talked to them about it. She remarked that the artist felt thankful to his grandmothers for guiding him when he felt frightened, such as when he traveled through the mountains. The teacher then pointed out how Littlechild used photographs of his grandmothers in his painting. At this point, a child in one of the preschool classes pointed to the grandmothers painting and asked, "Are they the bad people?" The teacher was a bit stunned since they had been talking about how grateful the artist felt toward his grandmothers. She replied, "No, they're not bad. They're his grandmothers, and they make him feel safe." Later, when the child's classroom teacher asked him why he had wondered if the grandmothers were bad, the child replied, "Because they have guns." Of course, there are no guns in the picture, just Indian women wearing shawls. Apparently he had such a strong association between Indians and warfare that he imputed guns into the picture.

On subsequent days, the children listened to the second Laurel Porter-Gaylord book, *I Love My Mommy Because ...,* and continued to talk about their families. They looked at other paintings from both the Littlechild and the G. T. Cunningham School books. On one occasion, while the children were discussing Littlechild's painting "Red Horse in a Sea of White Horses," the teacher asked the class how they thought it would feel to be the only red horse. One little girl replied, "I think it would be lonely." Having set the stage for the project by sharing and discussing the various books and by collecting photographs from each child's family, the teachers felt ready to expand the project.

Kindergarten

The kindergarten classrooms already had individual diaries for each child in place prior to the start of the project. At the fall open house, the teachers asked parents to send a small photo album to school with pictures of their child at various ages. The albums included comments from the parents. The teachers noticed an immediate resurgence of interest in these albums once the Family Heritage Project began. The children became much more aware of each other's albums and shared them with one another.

The kindergarten teachers initiated the Family Heritage Project following a school visit from artist and children's author Keiko Kasza. She explained a technique that she uses in her artwork that involves posing her own children in various positions, photographing them, and then drawing animal characters in her books in the same positions. To illustrate this technique, in each instance she showed a slide of her child followed by a picture from one of her books with the character in the same position.

Following the author visit, the kindergarten teachers shared selected pages from George Littlechild's book *This Land Is My Land* with their classes. First, the teachers reminded the children of the way that Keiko Kasza's family helped her with her artwork and stories. Then they explained that they had a book to share in which a Native American author's family helped him in a different way. With this introduction, they looked at the dedication page of

Littlechild's book, which includes photographs of his ancestors. In one class, a child commented that the people on that page looked bad, and Indians would scalp you. Several children immediately agreed, which prompted a discussion with the teacher. She told them that she has some Native ancestry herself, which seemed to cause some disequilibrium as the children tried to balance their negative images of Indians with their positive feelings about their teacher. Next the classes looked at the painting "Give Thanks to the Grandmothers" and talked about it. The teachers commented on the artist's use of photography in his paintings as they discussed the pictures with the children.

The kindergarten teachers also shared the G. T. Cunningham School book *We Are All Related* with their classes. Once again, they looked first at the dedication page, which is a reprint of the dedication page in Littlechild's book. As they discussed the artwork of the Cunningham School children, the teachers explained that the children had used the same photographic technique as George Littlechild. One of the kindergarten teachers remarked that all of the children in the book were older than kindergarten age, and she asked her students if they thought they could also use pictures and artwork to represent their families. The children enthusiastically accepted the challenge, and one child suggested that the teacher make lots of copies of their photographs so they could practice using them in artwork before they made their final pictures. In their kindergarten newsletter, the teachers asked parents to send family photographs to school so they could get started on the project.

Expanding the Project

Preschool

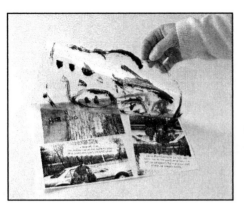

In Monica's preschool class, the children sorted through photocopies of their family pictures and decided which ones they wanted to use. Some children selected just a few photos, while others chose to use them all. The children mounted their family photographs on construction paper to create collages.

One child devised a way to glue pictures on top of pictures so they could be lifted up to reveal every photo of her family.

Next, using black acrylic paint on clear plastic overhead projector sheets, the children painted representations, ideas, or imaginings about their families. The painted acetate sheets were then mounted as overlays over the photographic collages. They were stapled at the top so the children could lift the acetate overlays to reveal the full photographic collage beneath them. This layered artwork proved to be very exciting for the children.

As one would expect in an open-ended, creative project, there were many different aspects of family life depicted by the children, as well as varying stages of drawing represented in their work. Many of the paintings were representational, while others were more free form. Irrespective of age or stage of development, all of the children took deep interest in the project. They wrote or dictated their reflections about their families after completing their artwork. One child, who had painted each member of her family, confided, "There's also a baby in the picture. You can't see it because it's not born yet."

In Lowellette's classroom, photocopies of the family photographs were first added to the open art area. Children could use them however they chose in combination with the other art materials. Next, the children each selected one photograph, which the teacher scanned into a computer and printed in color on clear acetate overhead projector sheets. After the pictures were cut out of the acetate, the children created collages by mounting them to the sticky side of clear Con-Tact paper along with small pieces of tissue paper. A second piece of clear Con-Tact paper was then placed over the top of the creation to preserve it. The tissue and photo collages were hung in the window of the classroom where the light could pass through them. This phase of the project was planned collaboratively by the teacher and a university art student. The children enjoyed discussing their photographic displays. One child commented, "This is me when I was a baby. I acted the way my baby brother do now."

Another university art student designed the next phase of this class's project. She printed copies of each child's family photograph in black and white onto clear acetate overhead projector sheets. Next, the

children dipped their hands in paint and made handprints on clear acetate paper. Placing a sheet of heavy paper over their handprints, they transferred the hand impressions onto the paper by rolling across the paper with rolling pins. When the handprints on paper were dry, the children used inked stamps to decorate around them. The acetate sheet with the family photograph was then mounted over the handprint artwork, which remained visible beneath it. The acetate sheets with handprints were used in the next phase of the project.

For the final phase of this project, the art student photocopied, in color, one family photograph for each child and trimmed around the pictures with deckle scissors to create a ragged edge. Next, she mounted the photographs to poster board, and the children created a border collage with sparkly materials, such as colored glue pens, glitter, sequins, spangles, and craft jewels. The handprints on acetate, created in the earlier experience, and the family portrait collage were then mounted back-to-back and attached across the top so they could be opened into a tent configuration and displayed on the top of a shelf in the classroom.

The Family Heritage Project was also incorporated into group time experiences in both preschool classrooms. Each day, several children read their diaries to their class during group time. This became a much-anticipated part of the day, and children were sure to remind their teacher when it was their turn. In addition, certain aspects of the project were integrated into the writing center of the classroom through the inclusion of small, teacher-made blank books with the phrase "I love my mommy because ...," which coordinated with the Laurel Porter-Gaylord books. The words "daddy," "grandma," and "grandpa" were included on some of the books. The children completed the books by writing about special aspects of their parents or relatives. To further encourage writing and home/school connections, the dramatic play area was transformed into a post office, and the children wrote letters home to their families on story paper, which is blank on the top and lined on the bottom. In this way, they could include a drawing with their letter. One class walked to the local post office to purchase stamps and mail their letters. Each child selected a stamp from the mail clerk and paid for it. Prior to mailing the letters, the teacher scanned them into a computer, reduced them in size, and printed them in color. After the post office trip, she mounted a copy of each child's letter on poster board, along with a photograph of the child purchasing his or her stamp, and displayed them in the classroom.

All my relatives live in Ireland.

Kindergarten

In the kindergarten classrooms, "represent" became the "word of the day" as the children discussed the colors and symbols George Littlechild used in his artwork to represent important aspects of his culture. They began applying these ideas to their own creations. For example, one child noted, "I used green and orange to represent the colors in the Irish flag. My family comes from Ireland."

The kindergarten classes combined photocopies of their photographs with a variety of art media over a succession of days. Initially, the teachers structured the activities so that the children used only one type of art medium with one photograph of themselves. This allowed them to explore the process of combining a photograph with each specific art material. Before starting each art activity, the children discussed who their ancestors were and what types of things they had done with them, heard about them, or learned from them. They were reminded to think about their ancestors as they worked. After completing each creation, they wrote or dictated their reflections about their family as represented in their artwork.

My dad told me a story of a fox. There was a big flood, and they had to keep going higher in a tree.

watercolor

The following is a list of art materials used in these explorations:

- Crayons
- Markers
- Print making, with spools and other found objects dipped in paint
- Watercolor paints
- Small die cuts of animals, fish, and other shapes
- Tissue paper scraps

tissue paper scraps

cutouts and markers

Once the kindergarten children had experimented with each type of art medium used in conjunction with a photograph, they created another picture using any or all of the art materials in combination with a photograph of themselves. The art materials were arranged in stations around the classroom, and the children were free to move from station to station. Finally, the children repeated the multimedia activity using photographs of their families. At the end of the project, each child's family portraits were assembled in a clear plastic accordion folder donated to the school.

Results

Preschool

Teachers noted many positive aspects to the Family Heritage Project. The diary display became the most popular area of the classroom, which led to many literacy interactions as children read and reread them to one another. Teachers also noticed that the children became incredibly interested in each other's diaries. For example, in Lowellette's class, the diaries were placed in baskets in a small reading area with two child-size couches. Children often assembled there to read them. On one occasion, when it was Michael's turn to read a diary to Amber, he read Carl's diary to her, not his own. Through their sharing of diaries, the children learned about many different cultures and families. They grew accustomed to talking about their diaries and came to expect that each child's would be different. In the process, they became much more verbally expressive.

Positive outcomes extended to the families. Many parents bonded and formed playgroups. Teachers noticed that parents became much more comfortable coming into the classroom, and they often stopped to look at the diaries and the panels that documented the project. Some parents began to arrive early at pickup time so they could sit and talk with one another. Parents also became more involved in classroom activities and were eager to share experiences from their own backgrounds and cultures. One mother made a piñata with the class, while another baked Argentinean cookies with the children and taught them two songs in Spanish. A father brought a book written in Mandarin for the class, and another father took a picture of the class with a camera he had received for Hanukkah. A mother and daughter came to school dressed in special clothes for Chinese New Year, and the mother later shared cultural information with a university class. When a new child entered the program, the first thing her parents noted was the class diaries. They immediately asked if their child could have one too, and her diary helped integrate her into the classroom. In addition to becoming more involved in the classroom, parents also began to evaluate Native American curriculum in their older children's classrooms, and think about aspects they may not have considered before. One parent brought in her child's elementary school social studies books to discuss the content.

Teachers also noted that the Family Heritage Project allowed parents of children who rode the bus to school to contribute to the classroom. Although they did not have a daily physical presence at arrival and departure times, they had a constant presence in the classroom through their photographs, messages, and stories. This provided an important means for children who rode the bus to connect to their classmates. It was a way for them to say, "I know what your mom looks like. Now you can see mine too."

Kindergarten

This reminds me of me and my dad fishing. We went down to Tennessee to fish. We used worms for bait and put the fish back in the water.

cutouts and markers

As the teachers watched the children interact with their photographs and the various art materials, they noticed that many children spent much more time on the Family Heritage Project than they would have expected. Some children who typically hurried through art activities added much more detail to their creations. For some children, the Family Heritage Project became a significant avenue of self-expression, and they were able to capture important memories. Some very quiet students verbalized deep thinking. The children never tired of the project and discussed their families in detail with one another.

Teachers noticed a resurgence of interest in the children's diaries once they started work on the Family Heritage Project. The children became interested in looking at each other's diaries, and the morning and afternoon classes began to look at one another's. The diaries were the first things that the children showed to parents when they visited the classroom.

Teachers found that the project was a way to connect home and school. They used digital cameras to document the children working on the project, wrote down the children's reflections about their families, and compiled the material into books that were sent home.

The kindergarten children seemed to become much more aware of artist techniques through working on the Family Heritage Project. In particular, they began to understand the use of symbols to represent aspects of culture or important personal

My grandma rocks me on a rocking chair.

markers and watercolor

markers and watercolor

experiences, and some children began to incorporate their own symbols into their artwork.

Since some families didn't send photographs to school, the teachers made pictures of all the children in the classroom available for use by all children during the project. Some children combined the photos of several classmates in their work and talked about special things they had done together. Picking up on this, the teacher asked children to use photos of the classmates they had been grouped with on a field trip in one of their activities. This drew children who typically did not interact much with one another into a closer working relationship.

markers

Reflections

The teachers involved in the Family Heritage Project are eager to expand it in upcoming years. In reflecting about their experiences, they have developed ideas for modifying and extending the family diaries and the overall project. The following are modifications various teachers plan to incorporate in their classrooms in subsequent years.

Preschool

§ Incorporate *This Land Is My Land, We Are All Related,* and *Rainbow at Night* more fully into the project by having them permanently displayed in the art or writing areas of the classroom.

§ Introduce additional art and music materials by Native artists.

§ Mail information about the diaries and the project to the parents before the start of school in a welcoming letter.

§ Have each family represented in the classroom through a photograph or some other material.

- Include a page in the children's diaries about their family's heritage or background.

- Include a page in each diary about a special family event, such as a celebration, holiday, vacation, or family reunion.

- Talk to families about the project on the initial home visit.

- At the beginning of the year, display documentation panels of the returning children's family-portrait artwork. Have incoming children create their own family artwork early in the year.

- Maintain the diaries and family heritage documentation panels throughout the year to establish a class history.

- Plan several family nights, with the first one centered on the family diaries. During the second family night, have the families work together on a project, such as a collage, painting, or clay sculpture. During the third family night, create family quilts.

- Combine journal writing with project work using a table in the classroom devoted to both.

- Invite entire families to the school open house rather than just parents. Encourage families to work on their child's diary during the open house.

Kindergarten

- Plan opportunities for the parents to explore the same art techniques the children are learning about. Allow the parents to then create the cover for their child's diary.

- Explore the project over the course of an entire year so the children can revisit it again and again.

- Find ways to encourage more parent involvement and more sharing of family photographs.

- Have the children integrate school curriculum into aspects of the project, such as drawing and writing about their personal experiences with butterflies when the class is studying caterpillars and metamorphosis.

- Find ways to use family photographs in many ways during the school year.

Conclusion

The Family Heritage Project succeeded in bringing children and families closer together and provided a real bridge between home and school. Perhaps one of the most important benefits of the project was communicating to families that their cultures were appreciated and valued by the school. Through the Family Heritage Project, teachers, parents, and children explored every family's culture almost daily, a much more effective and respectful approach than singling out one family or culture as an "oddity." Finally, the Family Heritage Project allowed children to more deeply understand the similarities and differences among families, including Native American families, and to be comfortable with both.

References

Hucko, Bruce. 1996. *A rainbow at night: The world in words and pictures by Navajo children.* San Francisco: Chronicle Books.

Littlechild, George. 1993. *This land is my land.* Emeryville, Calif.: Children's Book Press.

Porter-Gaylord, Laurel. 1991. *I love my daddy because ....* Pictures by Ashley Wolff. New York: Dutton.

———. 1991. *I love my mommy because ....* Pictures by Ashley Wolff. New York: Dutton.

Students of G. T. Cunningham Elementary School. 1996. *We are all related: A celebration of our cultural heritage.* Foreword by George Littlechild. Vancouver: Polestar Book Publishers.

Chapter 8

Guidelines for Teachers

Reflection from Guy and Sally

In 1996 we traveled to Dallas to give a presentation at the national conference of the National Association for the Education of Young Children. Prior to our workshop, we strolled through the vendors' marketplace looking at the materials being sold to teachers. We saw activity books filled with inappropriate "Indian activities," children's books with stereotypes of Native American peoples or misrepresentations of their cultures, and toys featuring generic "Indians" in headdresses and tipis. As Guy noted during our presentation, "We found everything we needed for our workshop right there in the commercial exhibits." It's been the same every year since. It became clear to us that educators need some guidance if they are to choose wisely from among the many materials being marketed at conferences, in stores, and through catalogs.

Principles to Guide Educators in Selecting Multicultural Materials

Our guiding principle in diversity education should always be respect for peoples, families, and cultures. We should continually strive for authenticity and developmental appropriateness in our curriculum. This means that for younger children, we select books and materials that reflect Native peoples today and integrate these materials throughout the year and in all areas of the curriculum. With primary-age children, we continue to follow these principles, but may begin to introduce some historical aspects of Native peoples along with historical references to other cultures or communities. Whatever materials we choose, they must be historically accurate, specific to a particular Native culture, and balanced as to point of view.

Guidelines for Selecting Class Guests

There is no better way to break down stereotypes and misconceptions about Native peoples than to have a Native American visitor in the classroom. Unfortunately, some cautions are in order. While it would be very rare indeed to encounter a person of European descent claiming Asian or African affiliation, such is not the case with Native American heritage. For whatever reason, many white Americans who have grown up entirely in the dominant culture seem to need to find some Native blood in their family trees. White Americans claiming to be part Native American, and therefore representatives of Indian "culture," abound. They are referred to by Native peoples as "wannabees." While it would certainly not be appropriate to put a potential classroom guest through twenty questions, some background information is essential in order to avoid more misrepresentation and inaccurate information. American Indian peoples come from specific Nations and cultures. They are not usually insulted when someone asks them their Nation, or tribal affiliation. The following are some guidelines for teachers to think about when selecting classroom guests and planning for their visits.

§ *Invite a Native visitor to class.*

You may get referrals from Native organizations that know Native people in the community. Avoid individuals who claim to represent all Nations. There are no generic Indians. Just as a visitor from France would not claim to know Scottish culture, a member of the Lakota Nation would not pretend to represent the Diné (Navajo) people.

§ Think about your goals for the children.

If you want them to build on similarities, consider asking your guest to just visit the classroom and "hang out" with the children. Children are sure to ask plenty of questions within casual conversations.

§ Seek out a guest who can add to your curriculum.

For example, if your class is studying community workers, seek out a Native American guest who is in a community service line of work, such as a doctor, firefighter, or builder.

§ Allow children to ask questions.

Most Native people are used to children's misperceptions. That's why they agreed to come to your class. Naturally we want children to be respectful, but a question such as "Why is your hair so long?" is not meant by the child to be rude. The teacher can facilitate by saying, "Are you used to men with shorter hair?" and then let the visitor answer the question.

§ Expect your guest to come dressed as he or she feels is appropriate, as would a guest from any other culture.

You may think that a jingle dress is really pretty, and perhaps you saw this particular guest wearing one at a powwow, but that is not the way Native people typically dress. Don't make suggestions that may offend the guest or mislead the children.

Guidelines for Selecting Children's Literature

Choosing children's literature that deals with Native peoples is challenging because of the large number of stereotypes that still appear in books, the numerous historical inaccuracies, and the number of authors attempting to represent cultures other than their own. Choosing carefully is crucial, though, if teachers hope to present children with accurate images of Native peoples and cultures. In many cases, teachers will find that they must replace some former favorites with better choices. For example, Sally used to include *Hiawatha,* illustrated by Susan Jeffers, in her classroom because she liked the illustrations and the poetic text. Later, after she became aware of the historical inaccuracies and misrepresentations, she replaced the book with a large assortment of literature by Native authors that appropriately portrayed their cultures and contained beautiful and accurate illustrations. A favorite became *Jingle Dancer,* by Cynthia Leitich Smith.

Fortunately, a number of excellent books written by Native authors are now available, but teachers may have to look a little harder to find some of them since many are published in Canada. The organization Oyate, listed later in this chapter, screens and markets books by Native American authors. Most of the books recommended in this work are available from Oyate. Many bookstores will order any book in print for their customers, as will Internet book companies. Below are some criteria to consider when selecting Native American children's books.

§ *Scrutinize the author's biographical information.*
Many Native authors will list their tribal affiliation. Other authors may describe authentic experiences with particular cultures, such as being a teacher for many years in a Native school.

§ *Look carefully for any stereotypes in the text and illustrations.*
Mono-dimensional images, such as warrior, princess, stoic, environmentalist, and primitive, should naturally be avoided.

§ *Avoid books that lump all Native cultures together into generic images.*
These are not authentic representations.

§ *Examine the characters.*
Are they real, with in-depth personalities? Books should not glamorize any group of people.

§ *Think about how the book relates to your overall curriculum.*
Does it fit into a more global topic, such as families, so that children can see similarities as well as differences among cultures?

§ *Resist highlighting Native American cultures as topics for study.*
Integrate Native books and materials all year, just as you would with other groups.

§ *Do not include books in your classroom that show children playing Indian or depict animals dressed as Indians.*
This degrades and objectifies Native peoples and cultures.

$ *Look for books that portray Native peoples today.*
Otherwise, non-Native children will continue to regard American Indians as living only in the past, or as living today exactly as they did a hundred years ago.

$ *Seek out books that represent present-day Native peoples for preschoolers.*
Children of this age do not understand historical references.

$ *Seek out books that are historically accurate and include a Native perspective on historical events or periods for primary-age children.*
Children of this age can distinguish between the present and history.

Guidelines for Selecting Toys and Materials

Teachers should integrate materials with Native content throughout their curriculum, but as with books, care must be taken when selecting materials. Many toys that have Native American figures or props present stereotypical, inaccurate images. Indian warriors are still prominent in toys that feature cowboys and Indians. Dolls often adopt the princess image, such as the "Disneyesque" Pocahontas or the "Native American" Barbie doll. Some dolls are essentially colorized white dolls, with Caucasian features and brown-toned skin. Block accessories often feature Indian villages that clump all Nations into a generic assembly of tipis, birch bark canoes, buffaloes, and headdresses. Despite the minefield of inappropriate materials, good dolls, puzzles, and block accessories are available. Teachers should use the same care when selecting Native American materials that they would use when choosing materials representative of any other group. The following guidelines may be helpful.

$ *Avoid toys that feature cowboys, Indians, tipis, and forts.*
They are almost always stereotypical and violent. We want to promote pro-social images in our classrooms, not violent ones.

$ *Buy quality multicultural baby dolls, including realistic Native American dolls.*
Include them in your dramatic play area all year along with dolls of other racial or ethnic groups.

§ Select multicultural toy people, puzzles, and games.

Make sure they include Native American families of today in a variety of roles.

§ Scrutinize games and puzzles for stereotypical content.

Don't assume that more expensive European imports are free of stereotypes. For example, a Ravensburger color matching game features Indian boys in feathered headdresses crawling around a tipi.

Recommended Children's Books

Selected Bibliography

Many outstanding books by Native authors are described in the curriculum chapters of this book. The following bibliography refers the reader to annotations of those books and also lists other recommended books not previously cited.

Earth Daughter, by George Ancona. 1995. New York: Simon & Schuster.

Ages 7–12

Description on page 91

Powwow, by George Ancona. 1993. New York: Harcourt Brace Jovanovich.

Ages 5–12

George Ancona uses photography to tell the story of a modern Native American boy who does traditional dancing at a powwow. Children first see him in everyday clothes and then watch as he dons his dance regalia. Because of the length of the text, this book is most appropriate for primary-age children, although younger children may enjoy the colorful pictures.

Ma'ii and Cousin Horned Toad, by Shonto Begay. 1992. New York: Scholastic.

Ages 4–8

Description on page 111

Crazy Horse's Vision, by Joseph Bruchac. 2000. New York: Lee & Low Books Inc.

Ages 6–8

Crazy Horse is one of the most famous heroes of American Indian people. This book describes his childhood, his strong relationship to his Oglala Lakota people, and the powerful vision he had as a child. The illustrations, by Lakota artist S. D. Nelson, are breathtaking. Abenaki author Joseph Bruchac has written many highly regarded children's books. At the end of the book, he gives extensive background information about Crazy Horse that would be very helpful to teachers. Since this book deals with a historical figure, it is best suited for primary-age children.

Fox Song, by Joseph Bruchac. 1993. New York: Philomel Books.

Ages 6–8

Description on page 77

The Story of the Milky Way, by Joseph Bruchac and Gayle Ross. 1995. New York: Dial Books.

Ages 3–6

Description on page 60

Foster Baby, by Rhian Brynjolson. 1996. Winnipeg: Pemmican Publications.

Ages 3–6

With beautiful, full-page illustrations, this book sensitively describes a Native American baby in a loving foster home that is also Native American. Children respond to the engaging descriptions and illustrations of the whole family interacting with this adorable baby. Foster care is a subject that is not often covered in children's literature. This book fills an important gap.

Abuela's Weave, by Omar S. Castañeda. 1993. New York: Lee & Low.

Ages 4–8

Description on page 57

Did You Hear Wind Sing Your Name? by Sandra De Coteau Orie. 1995. New York: Walker and Company.

Ages 3–6

Description on page 102

Chester Bear, Where Are You? by Peter Eyvindson. 1998. Winnipeg: Pemmican Publications.

Ages 3–5

Description on page 51

Kyle's Bath, by Peter Eyvindson. 1994. Winnipeg: Pemmican Publications.

Ages 3–5

Description on page 34

Old Enough, by Peter Eyvindson. 1993. Winnipeg: Pemmican Publications.

Ages 3–5

This intergenerational book shows a modern Native family. The father dreams of all the things he will do with his young son, but then becomes too busy with work to spend much time with him. It is only when he has a grandson that he makes sure he has enough time to enjoy all of the child's activities, such as sledding, flying kites, playing ball, and walking on stilts. The book has a limited amount of text and black and white illustrations.

We Are All Related, by students of G. T. Cunningham Elementary School. 1996. Vancouver: Polestar Book Publishers.

Ages 4–12

Description on page 118

The Good Luck Cat, by Joy Harjo. 2000. San Diego: Harcourt.

Ages 3–5

Description on page 41

A Rainbow at Night: The World in Words and Pictures by Navajo Children, by Bruce Hucko. 1996. San Francisco: Chronicle Books.

Ages 4–12

Description on page 94

Emma and the Trees, by Lenore Keeshig-Tobias. 1996. Toronto: Sister Vision, Black Women and Women of Colour Press.

Ages 3–5

Description on page 106

Baseball Bats for Christmas, by Michael Arvaarluk Kusugak. 1996. Toronto: Annick Press.

Ages 4–8

Description on page 42

My Arctic 1,2,3, by Michael Arvaarluk Kusugak. 1999. Toronto: Annick Press.

Ages 3–5

Description on page 88

Northern Lights: The Soccer Trails, by Michael Arvaarluk Kusugak. 1993 Toronto: Annick Press.

Ages 4–8

Description on page 78

Less Than Half, More Than Whole, by Kathleen and Michael Lacapa. 1994. Flagstaff, Ariz.: Northland Publishing Company.

Ages 4–8

Description on page 75

Byron Through the Seasons, by the Children of La Loche and Friends. 1990. Saskatoon: Fifth House Publishers.

Ages 3–6

Description on page 72

This Land Is My Land, by George Littlechild. 1993. Emeryville, Calif.: Children's Book Press.

Ages 4–12

Description on page 118

Nanabosho and the Woodpecker, by Joe McLellan. 1995. Winnipeg: Pemmican Publications.

Ages 3–5

This hilarious book by Ojibway author Joe McLellan imbeds a traditional trickster tale within a winter adventure of four Native children. They have gone out to explore and play in the snow, when one child falls from a tall tree. After making sure everyone is all right, Grandmother tells a trickster story, in which Nanabosho tries to catch his food the way a woodpecker does and also falls from a tall tree. Young children relate strongly to the children in this book.

Clambake: A Wampanoag Tradition, by Russell M. Peters. 1992. Minneapolis: Lerner Publications.

Ages 6–12

Through photographic illustrations and extensive text, this book describes the life of a Wampanoag boy and his family. The author, who is Mashpee

Wampanoag, shows how this family blends traditional customs with a modern-day world. Because of the large amount of text, this book is more appropriate for older primary-school children than for younger grades, although all children will enjoy the photographs.

The Sacred Harvest: Ojibway Wild Rice Gathering, by Gordon Regguinti. 1992. Minneapolis: Lerner Publications.

> Ages 8–12

This book chronicles a young boy from the Leech Lake Reservation in Minnesota as he learns to harvest rice in the traditional Ojibway practice. Children will enjoy looking at the clear photographic illustrations; however, the lengthy text may need to be reduced even for older primary-school children.

Two Pairs of Shoes, by Esther Sanderson. 1994. Winnipeg: Pemmican Publications.

> Ages 3–5

Description on page 37

On Mother's Lap, by Ann Herbert Scott. 1993. New York: Scholastic.

> Ages 3–5

Description on page 55

Jingle Dancer, by Cynthia Leitich Smith. 2000. New York: Morrow Junior Books.

> Ages 3–8

Description on page 68

Giving Thanks, by Chief Jake Swamp. 1995. New York: Lee & Low Books.

> Ages 3–5

Mohawk author Jake Swamp explains that Haudenosaunee (Iroquois) children are traditionally taught to give thanks to all living things each morning. While both the words and illustrations in this book are lovely, the pictures depict Native people of the past. This may confuse young non-Native children unless they have other materials that show Native peoples today.

Navajo ABC: A Diné Alphabet Book, by Luci Tapahonso and Eleanor Schick. 1995. New York: Simon & Schuster.

Ages 3–5

Description on page 89

The Big Tree and the Little Tree, as told by Mary Augusta Tappage, edited by Jean E. Speare. 1986. Winnipeg: Pemmican Publications.

Ages 4–6

Description on page 105

Cheryl's Potlatch, by Sheila Thompson. 1994. Vanderhoof, B.C.: Yinka Dene Language Institute.

Ages 4–8

Description on page 93

Firedancers, by Jan Bourdeau Waboose. 2000. New York: Stoddart Kids.

Ages 4–8

Author Jan Bourdeau Waboose is Nishinawbe Ojibway and a member of the Bear Clan. In *Firedancers,* a young Anishinawbe girl narrates a special evening she spends with her grandmother. Taking a small motorboat across a river to an island, they build a fire in an ancient clearing and sit together. Grandmother recounts the ceremonial dances she has participated in on that very spot, as did her ancestors. When the time is right, Grandmother pulls her moccasins from a bag and begins to dance. As the young girl joins her grandmother in the dance, she hears the drum and foot beats of her ancestors dancing with them. This lyrical text links past and present in the traditions of the Ojibway. The illustrations are colorful and should capture the interest of older preschool, kindergarten, and primary-age children.

Morning on the Lake, by Jan Bourdeau Waboose. 1997. Toronto: Kids Can Press.

> Ages 5–10

Description on page 111

SkySisters, by Jan Bourdeau Waboose. 2000. Toronto: Kids Can Press.

> Ages 4–8

Description on page 109

Andy, an Alaskan Tale, by Susan Welsh-Smith. 1991. New York: Cambridge University Press.

> Ages 3–5

Description on page 86

Where Did You Get Your Moccasins? by Bernelda Wheeler. 1992. Winnipeg: Peguis Publishers.

> Ages 3–5

Description on page 37

Problematic Children's Books

Selected Bibliography

Earlier we discussed problems related to books about Native American peoples written by non-Native authors or writers not familiar with the cultures they are representing. The bulk of the literature written about American Indians falls into this category, and most of the books have serious problems. Readers are strongly urged to review the books *Through Indian Eyes: The Native Experience in Books for Children* and *American Indian Stereotypes in the World of Children* (Slapin and Seale 1998) to gain an understanding of the tremendous scope of the problem. The following is a discussion of several problematic children's books. This is by no means an exhaustive list. Such a list would undoubtedly include scores of titles. The books reviewed are merely a selected sample used to illustrate the pandemic problems of historical inaccuracies, misrepresentation of Native peoples, and cultural stereotyping. We hope that raising these issues heightens the awareness of teachers so that they look more thoughtfully and critically at other books in the Native genre. When teachers are unable to accurately evaluate a particular book, we urge them to contact an informed representative of the specific Native Nation portrayed in the book. The Web site of the National Congress of American Indians, www.ncai.org, includes a directory of Indian Nations.

Friendship's First Thanksgiving, by William Accorsi. 1994. New York: Scholastic.

This book is an example of the distortions of history promoted in most children's books about Thanksgiving. The story is told by a little dog who supposedly accompanied the Pilgrims on the Mayflower. Indians are immediately characterized as dangerous and Pilgrims as good and spiritual. The Pilgrims land, give thanks to God, and hope they don't meet unfriendly Indians or wild animals. When they do see Indians, the Indians vanish into the forest, chased by the Pilgrims, who we are told only want to make friends. In actuality, the Pilgrims robbed Indian graves, stole seed corn, and kidnapped Indian people. As the book continues, we find that there was, in fact, a nice Indian named Squanto. What we don't hear is the historical fact that he was kidnapped and sold into slavery. As the story continues, the Pilgrims are so successful with their farming that they invite the Indians to a Thanksgiving feast and share their food, a reversal of reality, since it was no doubt Indian people who did the bulk of the sharing. The Indians arrive in their finest loincloths. (They never seem bothered by the cold November air.) As always, we learn that this was the beginning of a long friendship. This myth is a complete rewriting of history. Far from living in peace, the Pilgrims exterminated groups of Indians, took all of their lands, infected them with devastating diseases, and brought them to the brink of extinction. As an afterthought, the author tells us that the Pilgrim dog and an Indian dog had puppies together, and three were given Indian names, including "Chase His Own Tail." This book is derogatory and thoroughly inaccurate.

Brother Eagle, Sister Sky, by Susan Jeffers. 1991. New York: Dial Books for Young Readers.

There is no doubt that Susan Jeffers is a very talented artist; however, this rendering of Chief Seattle's speech raises some troubling issues. Native people are illustrated as generic, in a mishmash of dress and culture. Most troubling is the way Native people are always portrayed in the past. At the end of the book, with the forests clear-cut, a white family appears to plant a tree while Native "spirit" families look on. This book strongly reinforces the idea that Native people no longer exist. This is definitely not a message that we want to send to children.

Knots on a Counting Rope, by Bill Martin Jr. and John Archambault. 1987. New York: Henry Holt and Co.

This is the type of book that seems at first reading like a good Native American story to people who are not Native. A blind child recalls his history through the stories of his grandfather. Since the artist and illustrator are not Native American, teachers would do well in a case like this to read reviews by Native American educators or librarians. Slapin and Seale (1992, 182–84) give this book very unfavorable marks in *Through Indian Eyes: The Native Experience in Books for Children.* A major complaint is the dialogue between the child and his grandfather, which seems intended to sound stereotypically "Indian." The reviewers point out that they know of no Native people who talk like that. In addition, they comment that Native children listen to their elders and do not constantly interrupt them, as the child in the story does. Many alleged cultural practices are misrepresented, including the naming ceremony, the attire of the people, the way they wear their hair, and the way they talk. The reviewers remark, "The romantic imagery of this book is no less a white fantasy than the bloody savages of more overtly racist titles."

How Would You Survive As an American Indian? by Scott Steedman. 1995. New York: Franklin Watts.

Teachers often turn to content books such as this one in an attempt to give children factual information. Unfortunately, in many cases the "factual" information is inaccurate or misrepresents cultures. This book is misleading from the outset. There are illustrations of American Indians adjacent to the various contributors, leading the reader to assume that the contributors come from Native cultures. In fact, the writer, illustrator, and designer hail from Australia, England, and Scotland, respectively. The book places Indian peoples solidly in the past, in line with the other books in the "How Would You Survive" series: *As a Viking, As an Ancient Egyptian, As an Aztec, As an Ancient Roman, As an Ancient Greek, in the Middle Ages,* and *in the American West.* Note that Egyptians, Romans, and Greeks are labeled "ancient," implying that they do have modern counterparts. American Indians do not receive this distinction in the series. Even the table of contents is disturbing. It is subtitled "Becoming an American Indian," as though children can transform into American Indians by reading this book.

Warfare is portrayed as a way of life for American Indians in this book, as indicated on the back cover: "A warrior looks into a bowl of blood before going on a raid." The author writes, "All Indian men dream of becoming great warriors. From boyhood, they learn that bravery in battle is the greatest glory a man can achieve. Warfare between the tribes is a way of life, and every tribe has traditional enemies that it has fought for centuries" (36). Of course, European countries also have long-standing conflicts with one another and produce brave soldiers, but when are we ever told that warfare is a way of life for them and their greatest achievement? There are many other stereotypes and misconceptions in this book, such as "The Indians' world is ruled by spirits" (7). The descriptions of spiritual practice paint the picture of superstitious, primitive religious beliefs. Misinformation persists into the glossary. For example, one entry reads: "DAKOTA, the correct name for the Sioux tribe, also spelled Lakota" (46). In fact, Dakota and Lakota are separate branches of the same Nation, which also includes the Nakota people. Another entry informs the reader that the Kiowa "were the only tribe north of Mexico to keep a written history, in the form of pictograms painted on buffalo hides" (46). Many Nations maintained written histories. For example, the Lakota kept a winter count, which documented the most important events of the year. Needless to say, educators need to be cautious even when selecting books categorized as "informational."

Publications to Help Educators

Selected Bibliography

There are notable resources to help teachers gain information about Native American issues in education and make wise choices of materials. The following materials are highly recommended.

Rethinking Columbus, the Next 500 Years, edited by Bill Bigelow and Bob Peterson. 1998. Milwaukee: Rethinking Schools.

This book of essays clearly documents historical inaccuracies and myths that are replayed endlessly in school curriculum as facts. Topics include historical material about Columbus, a Columbus time line, information about Thanksgiving, the plague of Indian stereotypes, and many more. Of particular interest are ongoing struggles of Native peoples, such as the sports mascot issue, environmental concerns, and treaty rights.

Light of the Feather: A Teacher's Journey into Native American Classrooms and Culture, by Mick Fedullo. 1992. New York: William Morrow and Company.

Mick Fedullo has taught on many Native American reservations throughout the country. This book documents some of the challenges and accomplishments he has experienced in his teaching and the talents, resilience, and determination of the students and families he has worked with. Fedullo describes his initial culture shock when his dominant-culture expectations failed to mesh with the values of the families in his new environment. Rather than assuming that their cultural values were misplaced, as so many other teachers did, Fedullo instead began to examine himself. As he grew in awareness, his teaching strategies changed and his students began to excel. This book is fascinating reading for dedicated teachers at all levels.

American Indian Stereotypes in the World of Children, by Arlene Hirschfelder, Paulette Fairbanks Molin, and Yvonne Wakim. 1999. Lanham, Md.: Scarecrow Press.

This is an outstanding book for educators working in the area of anti-bias curriculum. It begins with a research study that documents children's inaccurate and stereotypical views of Native American peoples. There is a thorough discussion of misrepresentations and stereotypes in school curriculum, children's literature, textbooks, toys, movies, sports, comic books, and Y-programs. This is a valuable resource for college professors, classroom teachers, and university students.

Lies My Teacher Told Me, by James W. Loewen. 1996. New York: Touchstone.

This book is not intended for early childhood teachers; rather, it is an analysis of the embarrassing misinformation in standard high school history texts. However, since there is extensive coverage of Columbus and Thanksgiving, topics required in many early childhood curriculums, early childhood teachers may find this book very useful.

American Indians: Stereotypes and Realities, by Devon A. Mihesuah. 1996. Atlanta: Clarity Press.

This book is excellent reading for all educators. The author, who is a member of the Choctaw Nation and an associate professor of American Indian history at Northern Arizona University, details twenty-four stereotypes and realities related to Native peoples and cultures. Each juxtaposition of stereotype versus reality is followed by several pages of information. Readers will find this book easy to read and understand. It contains important and valuable information for teachers.

Growing Up Native American, by Patricia Riley, 1993. New York: Avon Books.

This book is a compilation of writings by noted Native American authors that describe the issues faced by young Native American children. It spans the generations through the nineteenth and twentieth centuries. Simon Ortiz, Ella Cara Deloria, Luther Standing Bear, Louise Erdrich, Joseph Bruchac, Leslie Marmon Silko, and N. Scott Momaday are some of the authors included in this volume. The readings help teachers begin to grasp the historic issues faced by Native children and families forced to adapt to another culture's demands.

How to Tell the Difference: A Guide for Evaluating Children's Books for Anti-Indian Bias, by Beverly Slapin, Doris Seale, and Rosemary Gonzalez. 1998. Berkeley: Oyate.

This publication is an excerpt from the much longer *Through Indian Eyes: The Native Experience in Books for Children.* It is a list of biases, stereotypes, and distortions in children's literature with Native American subject matter. The authors give clear examples of problematic material followed by more accurate or appropriate coverage of the same topics.

Through Indian Eyes: The Native Experience in Books for Children, edited by Beverly Slapin and Doris Seale. 4th ed., 1998. Los Angeles: UCLA American Indian Study Center.

This is an excellent resource for teachers looking for guidance as they select Native American books for children. It includes excellent essays on Columbus and Thanksgiving and discusses stereotypes and misrepresentations in literature. Especially valuable are reviews of many children's books and criteria for selecting books. There is also an annotated list of resource material.

Indian Givers: How the Indians of the Americas Transformed the World, by Jack Weatherford. 1988. New York: Crown Publishers.

This book documents the extensive contributions of Indian peoples to global food choices, democracy, modern medicine, agriculture, architecture, government, and ecology. Many teachers are unaware of the impact of Native peoples in these areas and will find that this book fills an important gap in their knowledge base. This is an excellent resource for teachers who hope to adequately answer the questions of young children and supplement the inaccurate and inadequate information in adopted texts.

Problematic Teacher's Guides or Activity Books

Selected Bibliography

Teachers must be very selective when choosing activity guides, especially those dealing with cultures they are not familiar with. Typically, these books purport to show activities that will help children "understand" and appreciate people from around the world, or in some cases, from a wide assortment of Indian tribes. Since no one author knows such an array of cultures well, the curriculum suggestions are often inappropriate and the background material inaccurate. What happens, then, is that teachers present activities that insult or degrade the very people they are hoping to help children appreciate. In the case of many Native peoples, the activities presented in the books trivialize sacred ceremonies or practice and clearly should not be transformed into arts and crafts activities. At the very least, such activities focus on exotic differences rather than building on similarities among peoples. Below are some examples of activity books that exemplify some of these problems. See chapter 1 for a more complete discussion of these issues.

More Than Moccasins, by Laurie Carlson. 1994. Chicago: Chicago Review Press.

This is one of the most disparaging books we have seen. It is filled with misinformation, such as "The Indians worshipped the forces of Nature." Children are taught to make costumes, such as paper bag vests, breechcloths, and headdresses, so they can "dress up like Indians." Other activities include making a "peace pipe" from a toilet paper tube, creating war bonnets, and carving fetish necklaces out of soap, all of which involve sacred objects or materials. Specifics as to why these activities, as well as others in this book, are so inappropriate are covered in chapter 1.

Global Art, by MaryAnn F. Kohl and Jean Potter. 1998. Beltsville, Md.: Gryphon House.

This book claims that children will learn to respect people from around the world by copying their art forms. In some cases, especially those drawn from Native peoples of the Americas, children are asked to imitate sacred practices or objects. While it is true that the authors ask children to use their own symbols in their artwork, to associate art activities with spiritual practices of indigenous cultures is to reduce the sacred to the mundane. It is not respectful.

For example, painting with colored sand is related in this book to Navajo sand paintings. The authors write, "Navajo medicine men of the southwest region of the United States were taught to make pictures in sand on a dirt floor. The pictures, they believed, would cure illnesses and lift curses" (125). Note that the reference is in the past tense, but traditional healing practices involving sand paintings are still very much a part of Navajo practice. Many Christian religions also have healing ceremonies, but teachers are never asked to have children create craft projects from such rituals. In fact, Europe is the only region covered in this book that does not have religious artifacts incorporated into art projects. Other problematic activities include making totem poles out of boxes, Inuit animal fetishes, and Aztec "sun god" masks, as well as artwork representing the Dreamtime of Aboriginal Australia and Zen meditation gardens.

The Kids' Multicultural Art Book, by Alexandra M. Terzian. 1993. Charlotte, Vt.: Williamson Publishing.

This is another activity book that turns sacred practice and cultural traditions into arts and crafts projects. Children are guided to make the buffalo skull from the Lakota Sun Dance, one of their most sacred religious ceremonies, out of paper plates. Other demeaning activities include making "magical power shields" from paper plates, totem poles from paper towel tubes, and Lakota-Sioux [sic] "charm bags" from scrap paper.

Multicultural Festivals, by Wendy Weir. 1995. Santa Ana, Calif.: Wendy's Bookworks.

This book turns sacred ceremonies from several Native cultures into craft projects. Included are patterns for Hopi Kachinas, totem poles, and the buffalo head from the Sun Dance, which trivialize these sacred objects.

Recommended Recordings

Selected Listing

While music is often referred to as "the universal language," the sounds of music vary greatly among diverse groups. Listening to the music of various cultures, including Native cultures, helps children develop a fuller awareness of cultural similarities and differences and fosters an appreciation of the many ways that people express their feelings through music. There are many styles and categories of Native American music. In addition to the traditional music unique to each Native Nation, there is a wide variety of contemporary Native music including flute music, folk, jazz, powwow, and eclectic music. The following list includes selections of various styles of music that may be especially suited to early childhood classrooms; however, it is merely a sample of the many artists whose recordings are available. As with all materials used in the classroom, teachers should examine and evaluate the recordings before introducing them. Samples of many of these recordings can be listened to over the Internet.

Native American Flute

The traditional Native American flute, made of cedar or reed, has a hauntingly beautiful and expressive sound. There are many outstanding Native American flutists. Their recordings may include traditional or contemporary songs. Children and teachers often find Native American flute music to be very soothing. Below are a few suggested recordings in this genre.

Dream Catcher, recorded by Kevin Locke (Tokeya Inajin). 1992. Redway, Calif.: Earthbeat! EB-2696.

Kevin Locke is one of the preeminent Native American flutists. This recording includes a selection of traditional songs from the Lakota, Dakota, and Meskwaki Nations. Accompanying the lovely flute music are sounds of nature, such as waves, thunder, birds, crickets, and frogs. Children enjoy the lyrical, expressive music on this recording.

Changes, recorded by R. Carlos Nakai. 1982. Phoenix: Canyon Records CR-615-C.

R. Carlos Nakai is an internationally recognized musician and a virtuoso on the Native American flute. This recording includes both traditional and contemporary flute music and features songs composed by Nakai on the Diné Reservation. It is a beautiful and expressive recording.

Crossroads, recorded by Robert Tree Cody and Xavier Quijas Yxayotl. 2000. Phoenix: Canyon Records CR-7041.

This recording blends Native American, Mayan, and Aztec flutes, accompanied by drums and chants. Both musicians are highly regarded. Children may enjoy the blend of flute and percussion instruments.

Vocal Music

There are naturally many different styles of vocal music among Native peoples. The following suggestions blend well into early childhood programs.

Peacemaker's Journey, recorded by Joanne Shenandoah. 2000. Boulder, Colo.: Silver Wave Records SD-923.

These original songs, sung in the artist's native language, tell of the historic Peacemaker, who helped bring peace to all of the Haudenosaunee (Iroquois) Nations. The music is lyrical and easy to listen to. While most children will not understand the words, they will respond to the soothing feel of the music. Since the songs are recorded in the artist's native language, this recording is a good counter to the inaccurate "ugh-a-wug" stereotypes children are often exposed to in Peter Pan-type recordings.

Under the Green Corn Moon, recorded by various Native American singers. 1998. Boulder, Colo.: Silver Wave Records SC-916.

This soothing recording includes lullabies from many Native Nations, sung in their traditional languages. Aztec, Kiowa, Taos Pueblo, Navajo, Cheyenne, Oneida, Hopi, MicMac, Salish, Pawnee, Comanche, Lakota, and Pequot lullabies are included.

The World Sings Goodnight. 1993. Boulder, Colo.: Silver Wave Records SC–803.

This recording assembles lullabies of thirty-three cultures sung in their native tongues. It includes a Lakota and a Quechuan lullaby.

Powwow Songs

Powwow music is performed for dancers in the sacred circle of the powwow, so we would not typically recommend recordings of powwow music for class-rooms. An exception is a recording by the Black Lodge Singers specifically for children. It was recorded to help Indian children reconnect with their cultures and non-Indian children begin to appreciate the sound of Native American powwow music.

Kids' Pow-Wow Songs, recorded by Black Lodge Singers. 1996. Phoenix: Canyon Records CR–6274, vol. 14.

This recording combines the traditional powwow style of singing with topics familiar to many young children. Songs include "Twinkle, Twinkle, Little Star," "Mickey Mouse," "Monster Mash," and "Flintstones."

Andean Music

A very identifiable style of music has risen from the traditional songs of the Quechua people, who are indigenous to the Andes. It is played on traditional instruments that include bamboo *zamponas* (pan pipes), *kenas* (transverse flutes), and *charangos* (ten-string mandolin-type instruments.) The music has a distinctly upbeat yet hauntingly beautiful sound that is very appealing to both children and adults.

Cumbre, recorded by Sukay. 1990. San Francisco: Sukay Records SUK–07.

Return of the Inca, recorded by Sukay. 1991. San Francisco: Sukay Records SUK–09.

This group of Bolivian musicians has become very popular in North America. Their music features excellent performances on the above instruments, as well as the *toyos,* which are pan pipes with tubes up to 5 feet long.

Eclectic Music

All cultures continue to evolve, and many Native American musicians are now combining the instruments and sounds of their traditional music with a wide variety of other instruments and world sounds. There are now concertos for Native American flute and orchestra, as well as jazz, folk, classical, and world-beat groups. Below are just a few suggestions from a vast assortment of music.

Feather, Stone & Light, recorded by R. Carlos Nakai, William Eaton, and Will Clipman. 1995. Phoenix: Canyon Records CR–7011.

This recording combines Native American flute, guitar, percussion, and vocals. It is a hybrid of musical styles that weaves flute melodies with jazz elements. This lyrical recording should appeal to many young children.

How the West Was Lost, recorded by R. Carlos Nakai and Peter Kater. 1993. Boulder, Colo.: Silver Wave Records SC–801.

This is music that soothes the soul, and teachers have commented about the calming effect it has on their classrooms. The recording combines Native American flute, piano, cello, oboe, violin, saxophone, vocals, and percussion in a beautiful, lyrical blend.

Clan/Destine, recorded by Clan/Destine. 1996. Phoenix: Canyon Records CR–7037.

This Native group mixes various styles of rock music with traditional Native sounds and themes. Some children may enjoy the upbeat rock rhythms and sounds. Of particular interest is the song "All Nations," which seeks to unite not only all Indian Nations, but all people.

Native American Artists

Selected Listing

Incorporating Native American art into schools and classrooms is an excellent way to educate children, counter stereotypes, and create an appreciation and respect for Native cultures. There are hundreds of highly talented Native artists. The following list is a sample of some of the artists whose work is available and may be affordable to schools or teachers. By entering the name of an artist in an Internet search engine, teachers can review examples of the artwork, review price lists, and place orders. Teachers will notice that in many cases artwork of other Native artists appears on the same Web sites. Thus, in searching for one artist, the work of many can often be viewed.

Artist: Wayne Beyale
Nation: Diné (Navajo)
Medium: Painting
Description: Beyale says that his work has been influenced by watching his father, a Diné Medicine Man, perform songs and healing rituals. He studied art at the University of New Mexico. Beyale blends cubist expression, lines, and nontraditional colors in his painting.

Artist: JoAnne Bird
Nation: Sisseton Dakota
Medium: Painting, Sculpture
Description: Bird studied painting and sculpture at the Santa Fe Institute of Arts, Macalester College, and Dakota State University. She describes her painting as coming from the subconscious and says she paints what she visualizes. In 1992 she was named Artist of the Year by the South Dakota Hall of Fame.

Artist: Arlene Kast
Nation: Apache
Medium: Dollmaking
Description: Arlene Kast comes from a family of artists on the San Carlos Apache Indian Reservation. Her unique dolls each feature some aspect of Apache culture.

Artist: John Guthrie
Nation: Cherokee
Medium: Painting, Sculpture
Description: John Guthrie often incorporates cast paper sculpture into his paintings. He represents the importance of a balance with nature in his artwork. Guthrie has received numerous awards, and his work is housed in many galleries.

Artist: Barthell Little Chief
Nation: Kiowa/Comanche
Medium: Painting
Description: Little Chief paints in both traditional and contemporary styles, and represents both Native American heritage and a devotion to endangered species in his artwork. He has received many awards, including the Grand Award at the Trail of Tears Art Show in Talequah, Oklahoma.

Artist: James Oberle
Nation: Cherokee
Medium: Painting
Description: James Oberle is the illustrator and cover artist for this book. Oberle's art reflects his Cherokee ancestry and a reverence for his people's strength and spirit. His art is housed in many fine galleries and collections. Oberle also illustrated the cover of the book *Animal-Wise* (Andrews 1999), and his work has been included in school textbooks and teacher manuals and has been recognized by national publications, including *Native Peoples* magazine.

Artist: Austin Real Rider
Nation: Pawnee
Medium: Sculpture
Description: Real Rider's imagery, based on Native American themes, encompasses the past, present, and future. He has won many best-in-show awards, including The Heard Museum and the Denver Trade Fair exhibitions. His work is exhibited in many galleries.

Artist: Eli Thomas
Nation: Onondaga
Medium: Painting
Description: Thomas draws upon oral tradition and cultural symbols of the Onondaga Nation, as well as a connection to the natural world, in his artwork. His paintings have been exhibited in Canada, Japan, Germany, and England.

Artist: Dana Tiger
Nation: Creek/Seminole/Cherokee
Medium: Painting
Description: Dana Tiger is well known for her paintings of Native American women. She comes from a family of nationally acclaimed Native American artists, and her family owns the Tiger Art Gallery in Muskogee, Oklahoma.

Artist: Johnny Tiger Jr.
Nation: Creek/Seminole
Medium: Painting, Sculpture
Description: Johnny Tiger is a leading Native American artist who has won numerous awards for his work, including Grand Prize at the Five Civilized Tribes Museum Annual Exhibition and first place at the Gallup Inter-Tribal Ceremonial Show. His works are housed in museums around the world, including the Russian Cultural Museum in Togliatle, Russia.

Artist: Donald Vann
Nation: Cherokee
Medium: Painting
Description: Donald Vann is a well-known Cherokee artist whose paintings have been exhibited at the Smithsonian Institution. His artwork has won recognition from the Five Civilized Tribes Museum.

Artist: Tillier Wesley
Nation: Muscogee
Medium: Painting
Description: Wesley has placed first five times at the eight Northern Pueblos Council Art Show. He has received numerous other awards, including Grand

Award Winner of the Trail of Tears Art Show in Tahlequah, Oklahoma, and first place at the Red Earth Art Festival in Oklahoma City.

Artist: Jim Yellowhawk
Nation: Lakota/Iroquois
Medium: Painting
Description: Yellowhawk is a nationally recognized Native American artist whose works have been chosen pieces for the Inter-Tribal Arts Experience in Dayton, Ohio; the program cover for the Tecumseh Outdoor Drama; and the United Tribes International Powwow. He has won numerous awards.

Publications

Selected Listing

Teachers often comment that they never hear news about Native American issues. Often the mainstream press does not cover these events. It can be very enlightening for teachers to hear news events from minority-culture press sources. Below are some Native American newspapers and journals that teachers may wish to consult.

News from Indian Country, Paul DeMain, managing editor. Hayward, Wis.: Indian Country Communications, Inc.

This Native-run newspaper is published biweekly. In contains news articles about Native peoples throughout North America, as well as reviews of books, recordings, and films. It is a member of the Native American Journalists Association, UNITY: Journalists of Color, and the Associated Press. The paper maintains a Web site at www.indiancountrynews.com and lists a subscription telephone number as 715-634-5226.

Indian Country Today. New York: Standing Stone Media, Inc.

Published weekly, this Native-run newspaper is owned by the Oneida Indian Nation but maintains offices throughout the country and covers news about all Native Nations. The paper was formerly the *Lakota Times*. It lists a subscription telephone number as 888-327-1013 and maintains a Web site at www.indiancountry.com.

Native Peoples, Gary Avey, editor. Phoenix: Media Concepts Group, Inc.

Native Peoples is a full-color magazine that focuses on Native American arts and living. Published bimonthly, it is available through subscription or on newsstands. The magazine is affiliated with the American Indian College Fund, Institute of American Indian Art, Heard Museum, Eiteljorg Museum, and many others. It features articles about artists, musicians, prominent Native American people, and history. It is an excellent source of color photographs for classroom use. The magazine lists a subscription number as 800-999-9718 and maintains a Web site at www.nativepeoples.com.

National Museum of the American Indian. Washington, D.C.: Smithsonian, National Museum of the American Indian.

This color magazine is published quarterly and is a subscription benefit for joining the museum. It includes articles that are both contemporary and historical. A recent issue covered powwows, Taino herbal medicines, play of the 1800s plains Indian child, Sacajawea's son, and an essay on Indian humor. A calendar of events includes exhibitions, public programs, films, and videos. The museum maintains a Web site at www.nmai.si.edu.

Web Sites

Selected Listing

The Internet is an excellent resource for teachers, but it is a dynamic medium. Web site addresses change periodically, and material on active Web sites is updated frequently. The following Web sites have material that may be especially helpful to teachers, including information about Native American peoples and listings of tribal organizations. Several of the Web sites are vendors who market Native American books and music. If teachers use the

Internet search engines to look for materials about Native peoples, they should use the same scrutiny in evaluating the information that they would use when selecting books or other materials. The guidelines for evaluating guests, books, and educational materials listed in this chapter may also be applicable when evaluating Web sites.

www.ncai.org

This is the Web site for the National Congress of American Indians. Founded in 1944, the National Congress of American Indians is the largest tribal government organization in the United States. Over 250 tribal governments are affiliated with the NCAI. It serves as a forum for policy development and works to inform the public and federal government on issues of tribal self-government, treaty rights, and federal policy issues that affect tribal governments. The Web site includes legislative updates, NCAI resolutions, a national calendar, and a directory of Indian Nations, advocacy organizations, and government agencies.

www.oyate.org

Oyate is a Native organization that evaluates and distributes literature written by Native authors. Many of the children's books recommended in this book can be ordered through Oyate. We strongly recommend that teachers consult Oyate's list of books. The Oyate catalog can be viewed on the Web site, as can reviews of problematic children's books.

www.canyonrecords.com

Canyon Records offers a large assortment of Native American recordings, including many of those listed in this chapter.

www.makoche.com

Makoche is a Native American recording company. It lists recordings by contemporary and traditional Native American musicians, including Kevin Locke, a Lakota flutist recommended in this chapter.

www.silverwave.com

Silver Wave Records distributes recordings by many contemporary Native American musicians, including R. Carlos Nakai, whose work is discussed in this chapter.

www.cradleboard.org

Cradleboard is a teaching project launched by well-known Native American singer Buffy Sainte-Marie. We have not reviewed, and therefore cannot comment on, the teaching materials. However, the Web site has an extensive listing of Native Web sites that may be useful to teachers seeking information on specific Native Nations and cultures.

Conclusion

We have decades of inappropriate practice to undo as we seek to improve the education of all children. Happily, we have many educators who welcome the challenge of reevaluating materials and teaching practices to better accommodate the needs of all children. We must all acknowledge that our children are our future. Through their clear eyes and compassionate hearts, which teachers, parents, and elders help them develop, will come a more honest and appreciative world for all.

References

Andrews, Ted. 1999. *Animal-wise: The spirit language and signs of nature.* Jackson, Tenn.: Dragonhawk.

Longfellow, Henry Wadsworth. 1983. *Hiawatha.* Illustrated by Susan Jeffers. New York: Dial Books for Young Readers.

Slapin, Beverly, and Doris Seale. 1998. *Through Indian eyes: The Native experience in books for children,* 4th ed. Los Angeles: UCLA American Indian Studies Center.

Smith, Cynthia Leitich. 2000. *Jingle dancer.* Illustrated by Cornelus Van Wright and Ying-Hwa Hu. New York: Morrow Junior Books.

Index

A

Aboriginal people, importance of appropriate terminology, xii
Abuela's Weave (Castañeda), 57, 62, 139
Accorsi, William, 146
Ackerman, Karen, 69, 80
Adamson, Melissa, 117
Adoff, Arnold, 76, 80
"African dust poses risk to health and ecosystem" (Schmid), 101, 113
A Is for Aloha (Feeney), 89, 97
Allard, Harry, 17, 26
Alligators All Around: An Alphabet (Sendak), 17, 27
Amazing Grace (Hoffman), 14, 26
American Indian. *See also* entries beginning with "Native American"
  importance of appropriate terminology, xi–xii
American Indians: Stereotypes and Realities (Mihesuah), 150
American Indian Stereotypes in the World of Children (Hirschfelder, Molin, and Wakim), 12, 14, 15, 26, 145, 149
Ancona, George, 31, 69, 80, 91–92, 97, 138
Andrews, Ted, 164
Andy, an Alaskan Tale (Welsh-Smith), 86–87, 97, 145
animals, books and activities, 86–88, 110–112
Animal-Wise: The Spirit Language and Signs of Nature (Andrews), 164
Annie and the Old One (Miles), 9, 27

A People's History of the United States (Zinn), 10, 27
A Rainbow at Night: The World in Words and Pictures by Navajo Children (Hucko), 94, 97, 119, 131, 141
Archambault, John, 147
Arlitt Child and Family Research and Education Center, 117
art and art activities
  class quilts, 58–59
  class stories, 95
  clay creations, 92
  crayon and watercolor drawings, 110
  creating toys, 44
  cultural insensitivity issues, 18–24
  display quilts or fabric, 59
  dream catchers, 21
  face painting, 22–23
  fetish necklaces, cultural insensitivity issues, 20
  kindergarten activities, Family Heritage Project, 125–126
  leaf tiles, 109
  magic power shields, 21
  Native American art, copying, not recommended, 96
  Native American artists, 95
  peace pipe, 18–19
  pictographs, 22
  preschool activities, Family Heritage Project, 122–125

sacred objects as school art projects ruled transgression of church and state, 24

sand paintings, 21–22

self-portraits, 76

sewing with beads, 39–40

Sun Dance skull, 19

totem poles, 19

watercolor paintings, 103–104

Art and Writing throughout the Year (Walrows and Tekerean), 79, 81

arts, books and activities, 94–95

art traditions

    books and activities, 91–93

    inaccurate curriculum, problems with, 10

Associated Press, "School scolded for Hindu dolls," 26

Aunt Flossie's Hats (Howard), 76, 80

authors' reflections. *See* Guy's perspective; Sally's perspective

B

Banks, Lynne Reid, 13, 14–15, 26

Base, Graeme, 17, 26

Baseball Bats for Christmas (Kusugak), 42–43, 45, 141

bath time, books and activities, 34–36

Battle, Monica, 117, 119–120, 122

Begay, Shonto, 111, 113, 138

Be My Valentine (Wigand), 14, 27

Best Best Colors (Hoffman), 76, 80

Beyale, Wayne, 158

Bigelow, Bill, 13, 26, 149

The Big Tree and the Little Tree (Tappage and Speare), 105, 113, 144

Bird, JoAnne, 158

Black Is Brown Is Tan (Adoff), 76, 80

Black Lodge Singers, 70, 80, 156

blank books

    Chester Bear, 54

    community animals, 91

    dancers, 71

    family seasonal traditions, 73

    trees, 108

blocks activities

    arctic animals, 87

Bredekamp, Sue, 12, 26

Bridwell, Norman, 17, 26

Brother Eagle, Sister Sky (Jeffers), 147

Bruchac, Joseph, 60, 62, 77–78, 80, 139

Bruna, Dick, 97

Brynjolson, Rhian, 75, 80, 139

Byron Through the Seasons (Children of La Loche and Friends), 72, 80, 142

C

Canyon Records, 163

Carlson, Laurie, 18, 19, 20, 21, 22, 23, 26, 152

Castañeda, Omar S., 57, 62, 139

The Cat in the Hat Dictionary (Eastman), 12, 26

ceremonies

    books and activities, 93–94

    inaccurate curriculum, problems with, 10

    totem poles, 19

Changes (Nakai), 154

Charlie Needs a Cloak (dePaola), 58, 62

Cheryl's Potlatch (Thompson), 93, 97, 144

Chester Bear, Where Are You? (Eyvindson), 51, 62, 140

Chief Seattle, 7, 147

children

    differences, appreciating, 33

    Native American perspectives, incorporating into curriculum

        bath time, 34–36

        nonrecommended activities, 44–45

        pets, 41–42

        shoes, 37–40

        toys, 42–44

    perception of differences and similarities, xiii

    similarities, building on, 32–33

    using counterimages to change perceptions, 31–32

Children of La Loche and Friends, 72, 80, 142

children's literature

    alphabet books, 89–90

    authenticity, need for, 9

    class stories, 95

    counting or alphabet books with stereotypical images, not recommended, 96

    dance books, 69

    families, 76

    inaccurate curriculum, problems with, 9

    problematic books, 145–148

    quilt books, 58

    recommended books, 138–145

    selection guidelines, generally, 135–137

    using as examples in text, xii, xiii

Clambake (Peters), 142

Clan/Destine (Clan/Destine), 157
classroom guests and visitors, selection guidelines, 134–135
Clifford's Halloween (Bridwell), 17, 26
Clipman, Will, 157
clothing
    brown bag vests, 23
    dance area, 70
    dance regalia, 20
    inaccurate curriculum, problems with, 10, 11
    stereotypical attire, displaying, not recommended, 44
    stereotyping, 14
Cody, Robert Tree, 155
Cohen, Miriam, 14, 26
Color Dance (Jonas), 69, 80
Columbus Day
    celebrations, inaccurate curriculum, problems with, 10, 11–12
community
    differences, appreciating, 85–86
    Native American perspectives, incorporating into curriculum
        animals, 86–88
        arts, 94–95
        art traditions, 91–93
        ceremonies, 93–94
        counting, 88–91
        nonrecommended activities, 96–97
    similarities, building on, 85
cooking activities
    popcorn, 60
Cooper, James Fenimore, 3
Copple, Carol, 12, 26
Corduroy (Freeman), 51, 52, 62
counterimages, using to change perceptions, 11, 25, 31–32, 66–67
counting, books and activities, 88–91
cowboys and Indians
    and children's fears, 2–3
    cultural insensitivity issues, 18
Cowen-Fletcher, Jane, 76, 80
Cradleboard (teaching project), 163
Crazy Horse's Vision (Bruchac), 139
creativity, books and activities, 57–60
Crossroads (Cody and Yxayotl), 155
cultural insensitivity, Native American issues in early childhood education, 18–24

culture
    stereotyping, 15
    symbols of, adopting, not recommended, 96
    traditions, misrepresentation, 9
Cumbre (Sukay), 156
cycle of life, books and activities, 102–104

D

The Daddy Book (Morris), 76, 80
dances and dancing
    dance activities, 69–71
    dance regalia, 20
    face painting, 22–23
    Native American dance regalia, 78
    Sun Dance skull, 19
dePaola, Tomie, 58, 62
depersonalization, stereotyping, 17
Developmentally Appropriate Practice in Early Childhood Programs (Bredekamp and Copple), 12, 26
Did You Hear Wind Sing Your Name? (Orie), 102, 113, 140
differences, appreciating
    children, 33
    community, 85–86
    the environment, 101–102
    families, 68
    Family Heritage Project diaries, 127
    goals for early childhood educators, 25
    home, 50–51
Diné (Navajo) sand paintings, 21–22
dramatic play and movement activities
    babies, 56–57
    campground, 73
    dance area, 69
    Family Heritage Project, preschool activities, 125
    Native American dance regalia, not recommended, 78
    shoe store, 38
    teddy bear interactive chart, 52
Dream Catcher (Locke), 103, 113, 154
dream catchers, cultural insensitivity issues, 21
dress. *See* clothing
drums
    Indian tom-toms, cultural insensitivity issues, 20
    stereotyping, 16

E

Earth Daughter (Ancona), 91–92, 97, 138
Eastman, P. D., 12, 26
Eaton, William, 157
The Eleventh Hour (Base), 17, 26
Emma and the Trees (Keeshig-Tobias), 106,
    113, 141
the environment
    differences, appreciating, 101–102
    Native American perspectives, incorporating
        into curriculum
        animals, 110–112
        cycle of life, 102–104
        nonrecommended activities, 112–113
        trees, 105–109
        winter, 109–110
    similarities, building on, 101
Eyvindson, Peter, 34, 45, 51, 62, 140

F

face painting, cultural insensitivity issues,
    22–23
Fairfield City Schools, 117
families
    consulting, for authentic cultural represen-
        tations, 49
    differences, appreciating, 68
    Native American perspectives, incorporating
        into curriculum
        loss, 77–78
        seasonal activities or traditions, 72–74
        self-awareness, 75–77
        traditions, 68–72
    similarities, building on, 67–68
family diaries, 76–77, 116, 120, 121,
    126–127, 128
Family Heritage Project, 116–130
    benefits of project, 131
    kindergarten
        expanding the project, 125–126
        future modifications, 130
        introducing the project, 121–122
        results, 128–129
    participants, 117
    preschool
        expanding the project, 122–125
        future modifications, 129–130

    introducing the project, 119–121
        results, 126–128
    purpose of, 116
    reflections, 129
    resources and inspiration, 118–119
    teachers' goals, 117
fancy pencils
    community animals, 90
    dancers, 71
Feather, Stone & Light (Nakai, Eaton, and
    Clipman), 157
feathers and headdresses, cultural insensitivity
    issues, 18
Fedullo, Mick, 149
Feeney, Stephanie, 89, 97
field trip activities
    potter, visiting, 93
    preschool activities, Family Heritage
        Project, 125
fill-in strips
    family seasonal traditions, 73
Firedancers (Waboose), 144
Flournoy, Valerie, 58, 62
food
    books and activities, 60–61
    containers with stereotypical images, use not
        recommended, 61
    food pyramid and traditional Indian diet, 5
Foster Baby (Brynjolson), 75, 80, 139
Fox Song (Bruchac), 77–78, 80, 139
Freeman, Don, 51, 52, 62
Friendship's First Thanksgiving (Accorsi), 146

G

Galimoto (Williams), 43, 45
Gilman, Phoebe, 58, 62
Giving Thanks (Swamp), 143
Global Art (Kohl and Potter), 19, 21, 26, 152
The Golden Picture Dictionary (Ogle and
    Thoburn), 14, 27
Gonzalez, Rosemary, 151
The Good Luck Cat (Harjo), 41, 45, 141
Gretz, Susanna, 17, 26
Grifalconi, Ann, 76, 80
group time activities
    preschool activities, Family Heritage
        Project, 124

Growing Up Native American (Riley), 150
Guback, Georgia, 58, 62
Guthrie, John, 159
Guy's perspective
    on acceptance of American Indian children
        into non-Native society, 84
    on community, 83–84
    on the effect of imposing another culture,
        1–2
    on the effect of terminology, 115–116
    on family structure, 65–66
    on long hair, 49
    on oral teaching, 99
    on people asking for information versus
        "stupid comments," 4
    on places of the heart, 47–48
    on teachers' guidelines, 133
    on teachings from nature, 99–100
    on terminology and discrimination, 29–30
    on trees and weather conditions, 105
    on where Indian people are in the world,
        115–116
    on wrong information in teaching
        materials, 5

H

Harjo, Joy, 41, 45, 141
Hiawatha (Jeffers), 135
Hiawatha (Longfellow), 164
Hirschfelder, Arlene, 12, 14, 15, 26, 145, 149
Hoberman, Maryann, 13, 26
Hoffman, Eric, 76, 80
Hoffman, Mary, 14, 26
holiday celebrations, societal traditions, inac-
    curate curriculum, problems with, 10
home
    differences, appreciating, 50–51
    Native American perspectives, incorporating
        into curriculum
        creativity, 57–60
        food, 60–61
        nonrecommended activities, 61–62
        nurturance, 55–57
        toys, 51–54
    similarities, building on, 48–50
homes, stereotyping, 13
Hopkinson, Deborah, 58, 63
A House Is a House for Me (Hoberman), 13, 26
Howard, Elizabeth Fitzgerald, 76, 80

How the West Was Lost (Nakai and Kater), 157
*How to Tell the Difference: A Guide for Evaluating
    Children's Books for Anti-Indian Bias*
    (Slapin, Seale, and Gonzalez), 151
How Would You Survive As an American Indian?
    (Steedman), 147
Hucko, Bruce, 94, 97, 119, 131, 141
Hutton, Mary Ellyn, 24, 26

I

I Can Count (Bruna), 97
If It Weren't for You (Zolotow), 14, 27
I Like You (Warburg), 14, 27
I Love My Daddy Because . . . (Porter-Gaylord),
    119, 120, 131
I Love My Mommy Because . . . (Porter-Gaylord),
    119, 121, 131
Inajin, Tokeya. *See* Locke, Kevin
Indian, importance of appropriate
    terminology, xi
Indian Country Today, 161–162
*Indian Givers: How the Indians of the Americas
    Transformed the World* (Weatherford), 151
The Indian in the Cupboard (Banks), 13, 14–15, 26
Indigenous people, importance of appropriate
    terminology, xii
Into the Circle, 71–72, 80
Isadora, Rachel, 69, 80

J

Jeffers, Susan, 135, 147
jewelry
    fetish necklaces, cultural insensitivity
        issues, 20
Jingle Dancer (Smith), 68–69, 72, 80, 143, 164
Johnston, Tony, 58, 63
Jonas, Ann, 58, 63, 69, 80
Jones, Guy W. (author). *See* Guy's perspective
Joslin, Sesyle, 14, 26
"Judge rules school district erred on religion in
    classrooms" (Zielbauer), 27, 97

K

Kachinas, cultural insensitivity issues, 23
Kast, Arlene, 158
Kasza, Keiko, 121
Kater, Peter, 157
The Keeping Quilt (Polacco), 58, 63

Keeshig-Tobias, Lenore, 106, 113, 141

The Kids' Multicultural Art Book (Terzian), 19, 21, 23, 27, 153

Kids' Pow-Wow Songs (Black Lodge Singers), 70, 80, 156

King Bidgood's in the Bathtub (Wood), 34, 45

K Is for Kiss Good Night (Sardegna), 90, 97

Knight, Mary Burns, 55, 63

Knots on a Counting Rope (Martin and Archambault), 147

Kohl, MaryAnn F., 19, 21, 26, 152

Kusugak, Michael Arvaarluk, 42–43, 45, 78, 79, 80, 88, 97, 141

Kyle's Bath (Eyvindson), 34, 45, 140

L

Lacapa, Kathleen, 75, 80, 142

Lacapa, Michael, 75, 80, 142

Lakota (Sioux)
   family structure, 65–66
   giving thanks, tradition of, 11
   preferred terminology, xii
   teachings on community, 83
   on truth about Columbus, 12

language. *See* terminology

Lauderdale, Lowellette, 117, 120, 123, 126

Lee, Jeanne M., 69, 80

Less Than Half, More Than Whole (Lacapa and Lacapa), 75, 80, 142

Lies My Teacher Told Me: Everything Your American History Textbook Got Wrong (Loewen), 10, 27, 150

Light of the Feather (Fedullo), 149

Lili on Stage (Isadora), 69, 80

Lion Dancer (Waters and Slovenz-Low), 69, 81

literacy activities
   teddy bear interactive chart, 52

Little Chief, Barthell, 159

Littlechild, George, 118, 120, 121–122, 125, 131, 142

living in the past, stereotyping, 15

Locke, Kevin, 103, 113, 154

Loewen, James W., 10, 27, 150

Longfellow, Henry Wadsworth, 164

Luka's Quilt (Guback), 58, 62

M

Mack, Stan, 52, 63

Mackey, Amy, 117

magic and mysticism
   magic power shields, cultural insensitivity issues, 21

Ma'ii and Cousin Horned Toad (Begay), 111, 113, 138

Making Music Your Own, 16, 27

Makoche (recording company), 163

Mama Zooms (Cowen-Fletcher), 76, 80

Martin, Bill, Jr., 147

mascots. *See* sports mascots

math activities
   bathtub game, 36
   doggie grid game, 87–88
   lost bear, 54
   lost cat game, 42
   neighborhood walk, 88–89
   recycling game, 104
   shoe collection, 38
   shoe graph, 39
   shoe patterns, 39

McClellan, Joe, 31, 45, 142

Merriam, Eve, 13, 27

Miami Council for Native Americans, 1

Mihesuah, Devon A., 150

Miles, Miska, 9, 27

Mimi's Tutu (Thomassie), 69, 81

Molin, Paulette Fairbanks, 12, 14, 15, 26, 145, 149

The Mommy Book (Morris), 76, 80

Moomaw, Sally (author). *See* Sally's perspective

More, More, More Said the Baby (Williams), 76, 81

More Than Moccasins (Carlson), 18, 19, 20, 21, 22, 23, 26, 152

Morning on the Lake (Waboose), 111–112, 113, 145

Morris, Ann, 38, 45, 76, 80

Multicultural Festivals (Weir), 19, 23, 27, 153

multicultural materials. *See* teaching materials

music
   cultural insensitivity issues
      drums (Indian tom-toms), 20
      rattles, 23

selection guidelines, recommended recordings, 153–157
  Andean music, 156
  dance area, 69–70
  eclectic music, 157
  music-dance video, 71
  Native American flute, 103, 154–155
  powwow songs, 156
  vocal music, 155
stereotyping, 16–17
My Arctic 1,2,3 (Kusugak), 88, 97, 141
My Ballet Class (Isadora), 69, 80
My First Picture Dictionary, 15, 27
My First Word Book (Wilkes), 14, 27

N

Nabucco, 23–24
"'Nabucco' research pays off" (Hutton), 24, 26
Nakai, R. Carlos, 154, 157, 164
Nanabosho and the Woodpecker (McClellan), 31,
  45, 142
National Congress of American Indians,
  145, 163
National Museum of the American Indian, 162
Native, definition, xii
Native American
  importance of appropriate terminology, xi, xii
  issues in early childhood education
    bias in schools, 3
    cultural insensitivity, 18–24
    diversity, understanding true issues of, 4
    goals for early childhood educators, 24–26
    inaccurate curriculum, 9–12
    omission from curriculum, 8
    outcomes for children, 24–25
    outcomes for teachers, 25–26
    problems in classrooms, 7–24
    stereotyping, 3, 12–17
    where to find answers about, 26
  perspectives, incorporating into curriculum
    children, 34–45
    community, 86–97
    the environment, 102–113
    families, 68–81
    home, 51–62
Native American artists, 95
Native American curriculum. *See* teaching
  materials

Native American Nations
  number of, xii, 10
  study of single nation, not recommended, 44
Native peoples
  developing accurate images of, goals for
    early childhood educators, 25
  importance of appropriate terminology, xii
Native Peoples (magazine), 162
nature. *See* the environment
Navajo. *See* Diné (Navajo)
Navajo ABC: A Diné Alphabet Book (Tapahonso
    and Schick), 89, 97, 144
negative stereotypes of Native Americans
  in children's literature, 147, 148
  clothing, 14
  in counting or alphabet books, 96
  culture, 15
  drums, 16
  as environmentalists, 113
  on food containers, 61
  homes, 13
  language, 13
  as monocultural, 3, 9–10, 23
  music, 16–17
  portrayal as animals, 17
  as primitive or living in the past, 3, 8, 15, 51
  recognizing and avoiding, 25
  sports mascots, 3, 61
  in teachers' materials, 152, 153
  use of term "red" to refer to Native peoples,
    12–13
  warlike, 14–15
  warrior images, 67
News from Indian Country (newspaper), 161
newspapers and journals, selection guidelines,
    161–162
nonrecommended activities (by topic)
  children, 44–45
  children's literature, 145–148
  community, 96–97
  the environment, 112–113
  family, 78–79
  home, 61–62
  teachers' guides or activity books, 151–153
Northern Lights: The Soccer Trails (Kusugak), 78,
    79, 80, 141
nurturance, books and activities, 55–57

O

Oberle, James, 84, 85, 159
Ogle, Lucille, 14, 27
Old Enough (Eyvindson), 140
On Mother's Lap (Scott), 55, 63, 143
Orie, Sandra De Coteau, 102, 113, 140
overview of text, xiii–xiv
Oyate, 136, 163

P

parents
    Family Heritage Project, interaction
        resulting from, 127
The Patchwork Quilt (Flournoy), 58, 62
Patrick, Denise Lewis, 38, 45, 69, 80
Peacemaker's Journey (Shenandoah), 155
peace pipe, cultural insensitivity issues, 18–19
Penner, Lucille Recht, 15, 27
Peter Pan, 17
Peters, Russell M., 142
Peterson, Bob, 13, 26, 149
pets, books and activities, 41–42
photographs, activities using
    Family Heritage Project
        kindergarten activities, 125–126, 129
        preschool activities, 122–125
pictographs, cultural insensitivity issues, 22
Polacco, Patricia, 58, 63
Porter-Gaylord, Laurel, 119, 120, 121, 131
Potter, Jean, 19, 21, 26, 152
Powwow (Ancona), 31, 69, 80, 138
primitive or living in the past, stereotyping, 3,
    8, 15, 51
purpose of book, 3

Q

The Quilt (Jonas), 58, 63
Quilting the World Over (Soltow), 59, 63
The Quilt Story (Johnston), 58, 63

R

rattles, cultural insensitivity issues, 23
reading activities
    likes and don't likes, 35
    toymaking, 43
    trickster tales, 112
Real Rider, Austin, 159

Red Dancing Shoes (Patrick), 38, 45, 69, 80
Reggio Emilia study, 117
Regguinti, Gordon, 143
religious beliefs categorized as myths, 79
Rethinking Columbus (Bigelow and Peterson), 13,
    26, 149
Return of the Inca (Sukay), 156
Richard Scarry's Find Your ABC's (Scarry), 17, 27
Riley, Patricia, 150
Ross, Gayle, 60, 62, 139

S

The Sacred Harvest (Regguinti), 143
sacred objects and symbols
    cultural insensitivity toward, 18
    dance regalia, 20
    drums, 20
    feathers and headdresses, 18
    fetish necklaces, 20
    inaccurate curriculum, problems with, 10
    Kachinas, 23
    peace pipe, 18–19
    rattles, 23
    sand paintings, 21–22
    as school art projects ruled transgression of
        church and state, 24
    Sun Dance skull, 19
Sainte-Marie, Buffy, 164
Sally's perspective
    on children's fears, 48, 66–67
    on children's reaction to "The Heartbeat of
        Turtle Island" (painting), 84–85
    on class diaries, 116
    on Indians grinding corn, 100–101
    on need to include Native American culture
        in multicultural education, 5–7
    on playing cowboys and Indians, and
        children's fears, 2–3
    on racism in play themes, 30–32
    on teachers' guidelines, 133
    on using counterimages to change
        perceptions, 31–32, 66–67
Sanderson, Esther, 37–38, 45, 143
sand paintings, cultural insensitivity issues,
    21–22
Sardegna, Jill, 90, 97

Scarry, Richard, 17, 27
Schick, Eleanor, 89, 97, 144
Schmid, Randolph E., 101, 113
science activities
    animal explorations, 112
    creating toys, 44
    grinding corn, 61
    shoe prints, 40
    spring in our community, 104
    Three Sisters garden, 102–103
    tree display, 107
    tree observations, 106–107
Scott, Ann Herbert, 55, 63, 143
Seale, Doris, 9, 27, 145, 147, 151, 164
Sendak, Maurice, 17, 27
sensory table activities
    bathing multicultural baby dolls, 36
sentence fill-in strips
    Chester Bear, 53–54
    community animals, 91
    trees, 108
Shenandoah, Joanne, 155
shoes, books and activities, 37–40
Shoes, Shoes, Shoes (Morris), 38, 45
Silver Burdett Music Centennial Edition, 16, 17, 27
Silver Wave Records, 163
similarities, building on
    children, 32–33
    community, 85
    the environment, 101
    families, 67–68
    goals for early childhood educators, 24–25
    home, 48–50
Sioux. *See* Lakota (Sioux)
skin color and appearance, stereotyping, 12–13
SkySisters (Waboose), 109, 113, 145
Slapin, Beverly, 9, 27, 145, 147, 151, 164
Slovenz-Low, Madeline, 69, 81
Smith, Cynthia Leitich, 68–69, 72, 80, 143, 164
social studies activities
    neighborhood walk, 88–89
    spring in our community, 104
Soltow, Willow Ann, 59, 63
Something from Nothing (Gilman), 58, 62
Song and Dance Man (Ackerman), 69, 80
Speare, Jean E., 105, 113, 144
The Spectrum of Music, 16, 27

sports mascots
    dressing as, not recommended, 61–62
    as negative stereotypes, 3
Steedman, Scott, 147
stereotyping, 12–17. *See also* negative stereo-
        types of Native Americans
The Story of the Milky Way (Bruchac and Ross),
        60, 62, 139
storytelling activities
    "Indian myths," inventing, not recom-
        mended, 79
    made-up stories, not recommended, 79,
        112–113
    tree puppets, 106
Students of G. T. Cunningham Elementary
        School, 118–119, 121, 122, 131, 140
The Stupids Step Out (Allard), 17, 26
Sukay, 156
Sun Dance skull, cultural insensitivity issues, 19
Swamp, Jake, 143
Sweet Clara and the Keeping Quilt (Hopkinson),
        58, 63

T

Tapahonso, Luci, 89, 97, 144
Tappage, Mary Augusta, 105, 113, 144
teacher-made materials
    stereotypical stickers, decorating with, not
        recommended, 45
teachers' guidelines, 133–164
    problematic guides or activity books,
        151–153
    publications to help educators, 149–151
    tourist curriculum, not recommended, 10
teaching materials
    children's literature, 135–137, 138–148
    classroom guests and visitors, 134–135
    evaluation, implementation strategies, and
        resource files, 25
    inaccurate curriculum, 9–12
    misinformation in, 50
    multicultural materials, selection guidelines,
        133–164
    music, recommended recordings, 153–157
    Native American artists, 158–161
    newspapers and journals, 161–162
    omissions from curriculum, 8

teachers' guides, 149–153

toys and materials, 137–138

Web sites, 162–164

Teddy Bears ABC (Gretz), 17, 26

Tekerean, Irisa, 79, 81

Ten Bears in My Bed (Mack), 52, 63

"Ten Little Indians," 17

terminology

    and discrimination, 29–30

    effect on thoughts about self, 29–30

    importance of, xi–xii, 12–13

    stereotyping, 13

    use of term "red" to refer to Native peoples,
        12–13

Terzian, Alexandra M., 19, 21, 23, 27, 153

Thanksgiving

    celebrations, inaccurate curriculum,
        problems with, 10–11

    historical distortions in children's
        literature, 146

This Land Is My Land (Littlechild), 118, 120,
    121–122, 125, 131, 142

Thoburn, Tina, 14, 27

Thomas, Eli, 160

Thomassie, Tynia, 69, 81

Thompson, Sheila, 93, 97, 144

*Through Indian Eyes: The Native Experience in
    Books for Children* (Slapin and Seale),
    9, 27, 145, 147, 151, 164

Tiger, Dana, 160

Tiger, Johnny, Jr., 160

tipis

    in classrooms, not recommended, 61

    as homes, stereotyping, 4, 13

    interpretation of significance, 47

tom-toms, cultural insensitivity issues, 20

totem poles, cultural insensitivity issues, 19

toys

    books and activities using, 42–44, 51–54

    Kachinas, 23

    selection guidelines, 137–138

trees, books and activities, 105–109

The True Story of Pocahontas (Penner), 15, 27

Two Pairs of Shoes (Sanderson), 37–38, 45, 143

U

Under the Green Corn Moon (sound recording),
    155

V

Vann, Donald, 160

The Village of Round and Square Houses
    (Grifalconi), 76, 80

W

Waboose, Jan Bourdeau, 109, 111–112, 113,
    144, 145

Waddell, Martin, 52, 63

Wakim, Yvonne, 12, 14, 15, 26, 145, 149

Walrows, Merril K., 79, 81

Warburg, Sandol Stoddard, 14, 27

warlike, stereotyping, 14–15

Waters, Kate, 69, 81

*We Are All Related: A Celebration of Our Cultural
    Heritage* (Students of G. T. Cunningham
    Elementary School), 118–119, 121, 122,
    131, 140

Weatherford, Jack, 151

Web sites

    Canyon Records, 163

    Cradleboard, 164

    Makoche, 163

    National Congress of American Indians,
        145, 163

    Oyate, 163

    selection guidelines, 162–164

    Silver Wave Records, 164

Weir, Wendy, 19, 23, 27, 153

Welcoming Babies (Knight), 55, 63

Welsh-Smith, Susan, 86–87, 97, 145

Wesley, Tillier, 160

What Can You Do with a Pocket? (Merriam), 13, 27

What Do You Do, Dear? (Joslin), 14, 26

Wheeler, Bernelda, 37, 45, 145

When the Teddy Bears Came (Waddell), 52, 63

Where Did You Get Your Moccasins? (Wheeler), 37,
    45, 145

Wigand, Molly, 14, 27

Wilkes, Angela, 14, 27

Williams, Karen Lynn, 43, 45

Williams, Vera B., 76, 81

Will I Have a Friend? (Cohen), 14, 26

Winnie the Pooh (Milne), 51

winter, books and activities, 109–110

Wood, Audrey, 34, 45

word cards

    Chester Bear, 53

    community animals, 90
    dancers, 70
    family seasonal traditions, 73
    trees, 108
World of Music, 16, 27
The World Sings Goodnight (sound recording),
        56, 63, 155
writing activities
    animal stories, 87
    bathtub stories, 35
    families through the seasons, 73
    giving traditions, 43
    likes and don't likes, 35
    lost toys, 53
    nighttime explorations, 110
    pet stories, 41
    special days, 93–94
    special places, 56
writing center
    Chester Bear, 53
    community animals, 90–91
    dancers, 70
    Family Heritage Project, preschool
        activities, 124
    family seasonal traditions, 73
    trees, 108

Y

Yellowhawk, Jim, 161
Yxayotl, Xavier Quijas, 155

Z

Zielbauer, Paul, 27, 97
Zinn, Howard, 10, 27
Zolotow, Charlotte, 14, 27

Other Resources from Redleaf Press